Christmas, 2001
İstanbul

To my beloved friends,
Who keep enriching my humble entity—

Cordially

Jyhan

LIVING POETS
OF
TURKEY

First published in 1989
ⓒ Dost Yayınları
Tünel Geçidi İş Hanı, B-Blok 9-210 Beyoğlu 80050 İstanbul, Türkiye.

ISBN 975-7499-00-5

Printed in Turkey by
Asır Matbaacılık San. ve Tic. Ltd. Şti. - İstanbul

LIVING POETS OF TURKEY

OF

TURKEY

An Anthology of Modern Poems
Translated, with an Introduction

by Talat S. Halman

 **DOST**
PUBLICATIONS

CONTENTS

We the undersigned certify that we have collectively selected the poets who are featured in this anthology.

Hilmi Yavuz   Cemal Süreya

Atilla Özkırımlı   Özdemir İnce

                    Salim Şengil

FOREWORD: ABOUT THIS ANTHOLOGY

This book is one of a kind. As its "Further Reading" section at the end will demostrate, there is an anthology in English that spans the entire lifetime of Turkish poetry. A number of books feature the selected poetry of individual poets. There is also an anthology composed of short stories and poems by 20th Century authors, dead and alive. This book, however, is the only one devoted to selections from the work of living poets.

Compiling an anthology is a task both arduous and thankless. Although as many as 28 poets (born between 1914 and 1944) are represented, the Editor is painfully aware of the injustice of omission perpetrated against dozens of other fine poets who merit inclusion. In a country like Turkey where poetry is a vital force and a popular pastime, there are so many good poets that to do justice to all of them one would have to publish many voluminous anthologies. The Editor, therefore, regrets the omissions and offers his apologies. One hopes of course that the damage may be repaired by other anthologies which might be produced by other translators or even by the present translator.

The selection of the poets has been made by three poets, Özdemir İnce, Cemal Süreya, and Hilmi Yavuz, literary historian Atilla Özkırımlı, and Dost editor-in-chief Salim Şengil.

The living poets in this book are arranged in chronological order, not in any hierarchy of importance, although it so happens that the oldest among them may be regarded the most widely respected in Turkey and abroad. For the readers' convenience, the biographical notes are presented in alphabetical order.

The "Further Reading" section is a simple guide for those interested in gaining a wider appreciation of Turkish poetry in the 20th Century, with some glimpses into its long past. My introduction attempts to provide a capsule description about the evolution of ancient, classical, folk, and modern verse. The readers interested in a deeper understanding will have to read other books, articles, and anthologies, some of which are unfortunately not easily accessible. At any rate, the listing in "Further Reading" is not a bibliography, but a sampling of reliable sources relating to modern Turkish poetry.

I should like to express my thanks to Mr. Salim Şengil, a highly enlightened publisher, who was kind enough to ask me to add such an anthology to his fine roster of books in English. My thanks also go to his charming daughter and efficient business associate, Mrs. Aslı Cansever. My friend Dr. Jayne Warner gave valuable help in many technical matters; I should like to offer her my appreciation. My wife Seniha T. Halman gave me her support and encouragement for this book as she has always done with my other books; my thanks go to her.

Like most anthologies, this book can be read at random, selectively, in piecemeal fashion - or methodically, in its entirety. What matters in poetry is the intrinsic pleasure the reader derives from it. If you read **Living Poets of Turkey** in full, you are likely to acquire a strong sense of the aesthetic and ideological concerns of Turkish poetry since the early 1940s. Also, you will probably gain insights into modern Turkish society and culture, because poetry is a faithful mirror in Turkey. Ultimately, this anthology endeavors to provide enjoyment, and I hope you will find some pleasure in it.

Talat S. Halman

INTRODUCTION:

POETRY ALIVE IN TURKEY

"Poetry alive in Turkey" is a truism which, although less compelling than in the preceding one thousand years, remains valid. The history of Turkish culture is intertwined with all varieties of verse - lyrical, didactic, epigrammatic, narrative, religious, philosophical, humorous, topographical, erotic, metaphysical, satirical, elegiac, panegyrical, and political.

Much of the legacy of poetry spoken, sung or written by the Turks in their ancestral Central Asian homeland, later in Asia Minor where they created the Selçuk Empire (mid-11th to the late 13th Century) and the Ottoman Empire (late 13th Century to 1922) survives although some of it has come upon hard times because of vast changes of vocabulary in the 20th Century. The poetry of the Turkish Republic (proclaimed in 1923 by Mustafa Kemal Pasha, later Atatürk) has been in the vanguard of the cultural transformation. It is both a beneficiary of the catalysmic changes which have taken place in Turkey since the 1920s and a forerunner of them as well as a moving spirit for them.

In the latter part of the 20th Century, Turkish poets moved towards a fertile synthesis of diverse themes, ideas and aesthetic approaches from their own Turkish background and from other cultures of the East and the West. Consciously or archetypally, this synthesis draws upon a complex legacy - Central Asian paganism, shamanistic Turkic culture, Arabo-Persian Islamic civilization, ancient Anatolian heritage, Selçuk and Ottoman Empires, modern European and American influences. Standing at the crossroads of diverse civilizations, Turkey has absorbed a vast variety of their images, concepts, themes and techniques.

The wellspring of Turkish poetic tradition dates from the second half of the 11th Century on the basis of written works, but probably much earlier as far as oral literature goes. Two major works stand out in the earliest phase: **Kutadgu Bilig** (Engl. tr. **Wisdom of Royal Glory**) by Yusuf Has Hacib, a mirror for princes in some 6500 couplets, and **Divan ü Lûgat-it Türk** (Turkish Compendium and Lexicon) by Mahmud of Kashgar, which contains scores of specimens of verses from the oral tradition of a thousand years ago. The major Turkish national epic, **The Tales of Dede Korkut** (twice translated into English), has long poetic passages and has been an inspiration to modern poets and playwrights.

In Asia Minor, Selçuks produced religious works patterned after Arabic and Persian literature in addition to the simple verses of the Turkish nomadic tradition. Islamic mysticism was pervasive in the work of Mevlana Celaleddin Rumi, the prominent sufi thinker and poet, and Yunus Emre, probably the most important Turkish folk poet.

One of Yunus Emre's celebrated poems (in syllabic verse) is an exploration of mystical values and the virtues of love and peace in a humanistic context:

God permeates the whole wide world,
Yet His truth is revealed to none.
You better seek Him in yourself,
You and He aren't apart - you're one.

The other world lies beyond sight.
Here on earth ve must live upright.
Exile is torment, pain, and blight.
No one comes back once he is gone.

Come, let us all be friends for once,
Let us make life easy on us,
Let us be lovers and loved ones,
The earth shall be left to no one.

To you, what Yunus says is clear,
Its meaning is in your heart's ear;
We should all live the good life here,
Because nobody will live on.

The Ottoman state, from the beginning of the 14th Century to the middle of the 19th, nurtured its court poetry and folk poetry, which developed without interacting. The former was an urban phenomenon, written by and for an elite, upholding the values of the conservative establishment, highly formalistic, abstruse, ornate in style, and classical. The latter represented the rural sensibilities; it stressed simplicity of style, lilting rhythms, and an easy lyric flow. Court poetry remained under the impact of Arabo-Persian Islamic literature while folk verse perpetuated the aesthetics of Turkish culture since pre-Islamic times.

The Ottoman classical tradition benefited from the patronage of the Sultans, many of whom wrote poetry themselves. The most prolific among them was Süleyman the Magnificent who composed close to three thousand highly structured romantic verses:

No end to this separation, no limit to this cruel
      pain -
If your gaze strikes to kill, the heart is willing,
      it will not complain.

My darling, your lovelock makes a long story out
      of my distress;
Tell it until doomsday, it will not end. Telling it
      is in vain.

Don't think the arrow of your gaze has opened
      a festering wound:
The heart has thus had its wish, the soul found
      its comfort and gain.

This has long been a custom among those beauties
      with moon faces:
First they give pleasure to your heart, then they
      start their torture and bane.

Our love asked about us: "Which one of the dogs
      is he at our door?"
May she live long, she gives us her respect and
      protection again.

This lover opened up the vast country of the
      heart to plunder -
Ah, the soldiers of distress raided and pillaged
      that whole terrain.

The second half of the 19th Century witnessed the emergence of "Europeanized" Ottoman literature under French influence. Since then, Turkish writers have used many European, British, and American models. Virtually all of the literary movements of the West have made inroads into Turkey. Westernization gained momentum following the establishment of the Republic in 1923 and exerted a profound impact. Looking back on Turkish literature of the 20th Century, one can define it as an extension of the literature of the Western world - with many dimensions from the cultural and literary legacy of the Turks dating back at least a millennium.

The far-reaching transformation brought about by Mustafa Kemal Atatürk and most of the leaders of the succeeding periods stimulated and was itself spurred by modern poetry. Poets stood at the vanguard of cataclysmic changes including a new political system, secularization of government and education, overhaul of the legal system, adoption of the Latin alphabet to replace the Arabic script, abolition of many Islamic elements, Westernization of education and cultural institutions, etc. The language reform which, in addition to the new Latin-type script, "purified" the vocabulary by eliminating words borrowed from Arabic and Persian and by reviving old words or by coining new ones, forced the poets to create a new style based on a fresh vocabulary and a new structure of rhythm and euphony.

It can be stated with assurance that seldom in history were poets confronted with a broader spectrum of change in such a short period and responded in a more enthusiastic spirit of literary innovation. From the early 1920s onwards, many non-Turkish literary movements and poetic innovations erupted on the scene - Mayakovsky-type free verse, Marxist-Leninist literature, Dadaism, léttrisme, Surrealism, Neo-Symbolism, obscurantism, actually any poetic approach that had gained ascendancy in the West. In the theory and practice of modern Turkish poetry, the prominent names of international literature - Valéry, T.S. Eliot, Pound, Stevens, Prévert, Brecht, Aragon, Apollinaire, Lorca, Breton, Laforgue, Eluard, Yesenin and countless others - became an important source of inspiration for ambitious exploration.

It was Nazım Hikmet (1902-1963) who revolutionized Turkish poetry in the 1920s with his firebrand Communist poems composed in lilting free verse and in a style that represented a complete departure from the conventions of the past. His influence still dominates particularly the poetry of the socialists and millenarian revolutionaries.

Nazım Hikmet brought to Turkish poetry a new sense of the joy of living and an optimism for a better world as evinced by the following excerpt from his book-length "Letters to Taranta-Babu":

the pomegranate that gives fruit once a year
    can yield fruit a thousand times

and the world is so huge
so lovely
    its shores are so endless

that every night
    we can all lie side by side on the gilded sand
    and listen
        to the song of the starry waters...

what a lovely thing to be alive
    Taranta-Babu
        living is such a beautiful thing...

To live
    as one divines a masterpiece
    as one hears a song of love
    as a child caught in wonder...

Traditionalist poets, too, have been revered by the poetry-reading public even if, because of the intractable difficulties involved in translating strictly stanzaic rhymed verse, they are virtually unknown outside Turkey. Among them are Mehmet Akif Ersoy (d. 1936) and Yahya Kemal Beyatlı (d. 1958), both of whom kept alive the strengths of classical verse and the conservative concepts of Islam and nationalism.

Mehmet Akif Ersoy, who wrote the poem which serves as the words for the Turkish national anthem, is famous for his patriotic poems, including "For the Martyrs at the Dardanelles":

Soldier, for these hallowed lands, now on this land you
    lie dead.
Your forebears may well lean from Heaven to kiss your
    forehead.
How mighty you are, you safeguard our True Faith with
    your blood;
Your glory is shared by the braves of the Prophet of God.
Who could dig the grave that will not be too narrow
    for you?
If we should bury you in history, you would break through.
That book cannot hold your epochs with all their
    rampages:

You could only be contained by everlasting ages.
If I could set up the Kaaba at the head of your pit
And carve on it the inspiration that stirs my spirit;
If I could seize the firmament with all the stars within,
And then lay it as a pall over your still bleeding coffin;
If I could hitch spring clouds as ceiling for your
     open tomb,
Hang the Pleiades' seven lamps in your mausoleum,
As you lie drenched in your own blood under the
     chandelier;
If I could drag the moonlight out of night into your bier
To stand guard by you as custodian until Doomsday;
If I could fill your chandelier with dawn's eternal ray,
And wrap your wound at dusk with the sunset's
     silken glory --
I still cannot say I have done something for your memory.

It is since the end of World War II that Turkish poetry has engaged in its feverish search for both modernity and sui generis identity. In the 1940s, Orhan Veli Kanık (1914-1950), Oktay Rifat (1914-1988), and Melih Cevdet Anday (1915-) brought about a further poetic revolution by simplifying poetic diction and democratizing the functions of poetry. Since the premature death of Kanık, Turkish poets have, on the whole, moved towards a fertile complexity. The so-called "Second New" school (the first presumably is the Kanık school) from the late 1950s to the early 1970s engendered a compelling Neo-Surrealism with a remarkable richness of vocabulary and emotional impact.

The transformation from Kanık's simplicity to the complexity of Edip Cansever (1928-1986) is startling as well as significant. First, Kanık's three-liner, "For the Homeland", which has become a proverb in its own right:

All the things we did for our country.
Some of us died,
Some of us gave speeches.

Cansever, one of the proponents of the "Second New", starts a fairly long poem entitled "Vanish" with the following imaginative lines:

I reiterate: your face is a laughter
Glance and an armada of life marches into light
A flower that hails from subterranean regions
An eagle gone starknaked
Now pink is pursued by three persons
Upward along your shoulder
Drive them insane in your hair
Carnation multiple
Carnation shrinking shrunk

The work of Turkey's living poets, represented in this volume by scores of selections, speaks for itself. It is a prism that emits innumerable types of light. It embodies a unique synthesis which is rich in its literary and cultural elements and promises to gain greater diversity as it voraciously explores uncharted territories.

GUIDE TO TURKISH SPELLING
AND PRONUNCIATION

For Turkish authors, names of places, and special terms, this anthology employs standard Turkish spelling. The modern Turkish alphabet appears below with a simple guide to pronunciation:

a   (like **gun**)   var. â (like **are**)
b   (as in English)
c   (like **jade**)
ç   (like **chin**)
d   (as in English)
e   (like **pen**)
f   (as in English)
g   (**g** of **good**)
ğ   (makes a preceding vowel longer)
h   (**h** of **half**)
ı   (like the second vowel of **portable**)
i   (like **it**)   var. î (like **eat**)
j   (like **measure**)
k   (**k** of **king**)
l   (as in English)
m   (as in English)
n   (as in English)
o   (like **eau** in French)
ö   (like **bird** or French **deux**)
p   (as in English)
r   (**r** of **rust**)
s   (**s** of **sun**)
ş   (**sh** of **shine**)
t   (as in English)
u   (like **pull**)   var. û (like **pool**)
ü   (like **tu** in French)
v   (as in English)
y   (**y** of **you**)
z   (as in English)

20

Of the twenty-nine characters in the Turkish alphabet, six do not exist in English: ç, ğ, ı, ö, ş, ü. The letters q, w, x are not in the Turkish alphabet although they may occur in foreign names. The letter ğ has its own capital Ğ, but never starts a word. The undotted ı and the dotted i are separate vowels whose distinctions are strictly observed in pronunciation and spelling. These two letters have their individual capitals as well: I and İ respectively. (The names of the cities of Istanbul and Izmir, commonly spelled with İ in Turkish, are spelled in this book as they normally are in English, that is with an I.)

SELECTED POEMS
(In chronological order by the
birth-years of the poets)

FAZIL HÜSNÜ DAĞLARCA

WORLDWIDE

Here or in India or in Africa
All things resemble each other.
Here or in India or in Africa
We feel the same love for grains,
Before death we tremble together.

Whatever tongue he may speak,
His eyes will utter the meaning.
Whatever tongue he may speak,
I hear the same winds
That he is gleaning.

We humans have fallen apart.
Boundaries of land split our mirth.
We humans have fallen apart.
Yet birds are brothers in the sky,
And wolves on the earth.

- The title has a double meaning: It could also be rendered
  as "The Language of the World" or "Universal Language".

ENDLESS SILENCE

I am like a brother to you well yes you can tell me
How you got married
How you stopped loving one night
All right you can tell me

And then in the days of that old photograph
Your Mother had not gone mad yet
Your hair was golden as it caressed your white
        shoulders
All right you can tell me

You used to laugh a lot
At trees
You were a sylph the forest kept you awake when it
        sprouted
All right you can tell me

Then you ran away from home
To thoughts solitude sleep death
Starknaked among the ruins of a fire
All right you can tell me

A girl a boy stone shadows on the walls a girl a boy
Three hundred youths you had slept in a mountain
        shelter
Outside the snow was cold as wolves in your heart you
        froze like the stone age
All right you can tell me

Look tomorrow I am leaving for another darkness
Like cemeteries I am silent mournful deaf
Yes you no longer have faith in love yes you will love
        no one ever again
All right you can tell me

GLEAM IN TIME

I am in the dark, beyond all light:
End of World War Two, ominous and heroic.
Far away slave nations chant a song.
I am aware of being a Turk.

A breath descends from the worlds across,
And shadows pour from time.
Upon the earth and over the atmosphere
I am aware of my chilly night.

Forms cuddle the houses and furniture.
What never was now comes into being,
And shapes border on eternity.
I am aware of my mind.

Not a tree grows with my seasons,
Nor are the stars as real as my own light.
Atoms astir by love fly in my heart every which way.
I am aware of life.

IS

To love
Is
To double
The world

WHEN I ARRIVE

Wherever I arrive
Day or night I see
My loved one
Has already arrived

TAKEN BUT NOT GIVEN

Hills and rocks
Left you to me
I shall not let anyone have you
Not even God

LANGUAGE OF POETRY

To write poetry
Is to speak the ultimate language
Not even God knows
All the languages the poet speaks

ELEGIAC PAIN

I am in such darkness
The night
Fails
Me

HOPE

Here
I believe
There
The bird flies

IT COMES AND GOES

It comes and goes
Till nights turn into dawn
My sleeplessness
To your beauty

HOW CAN I

How can I die
When a mad bird
On a mad branch
Twitters

BEYOND

Whenever I love a woman
I feel deep in my heart
That before me
God loved her

INSIDE AND OUT

Why are we separated
By houses
And come together
In streets

AUDIENCE

I am Halim the Third, majestic and sacred,
King of Kings.
When my white hands move,
My subjects come upon their mornings.

The moments I conquer carry my lust
To unknown virgins time and again;
I discovered time in the golden pleasure
Of my enduring reign.

Along my wisdom they stretch,
All the world's dimensions;
Comfort flows from my body
Into my palaces and stately mansions.

In legion with the mighty eagles,
I set science, poetry and victory free
So that generations to come
May rejoice on land and sea.

Dark-ridden and blue, heavens lie
At the beck and call of my head;
Poised as two infinities,
My love equals my blood.

Noble and hale, glorious and supreme,
Farther than the mind's eye can see through,
I am Halim the Third.
Mountains and rocks, who are you?

AWAKE

That we are brothers, that we are brothers
At the breasts of fire and air and mothers
Boy or girl, in an idiot's dream,
How does it escape us all
As the rivers roll?

That we are brothers, that we are brothers
As wheat grows green,
Lonelier than animals,
How is it we don't know, for heaven's sake,
The trees whisper it till daybreak?

That we are brothers, that we are brothers
The same star is fate to us and to others
Since the first darkness of the earth,
It escapes us all, why,
Though we keep staring at the sky?

IN PASSAGE

Beneath the giant stars our world is tiny
And our home a miniature.
Wild flowers cast their spell before dawn
Without memories or sleep.
Mint is their lure.

Everyone is in a trance since bygone days.
All things, in a way, are in rapture.
The coy mistress is divined in the girding space.
In the air the birds glide with love,
And the skies change in grandeur.

The heart observes nothing.
Its madness is pure.
Through our body and soul
Time passes
With its total torture!

GRAVE QUESTION

The west wind soared high as the mountains
Spreading
Silence
All over the earth.
Why say the dead sniver?
Have you ever slept the sleep of death?

In the forest syllable by syllable
Leaves gave you the mighty darkness.
Your body stood
Night by night beyond beauty.
Why say dreams are white?
Have you ever slept the sleep of death?

Shadows grew into the winds.
Brooks
And birds scuttled through your land.
Desolate lay the village road.
Why say your loved ones are gone?
Have you ever slept the sleep of death?

RETURN

Soldiers are returning, aged soldiers
From the blue hills of peace.
How intimate within our hearts
What their steps would not release...

Songs are returning, songs of light
Sung on hulky ox-carts.
Are the gardens across a mirror
Some new destiny that starts?

Birds are returning, loyal birds,
For our eaves, not for the sake of spring.
We come alive in the whirling distance
And the beauty that the seasons bring.

Ships are returning, strange and opulent,
Sailing the strange and endless seas.
In the depths, like beams of light,
The cargo of the ships tarries.

Unlike any of these, my night,
You, you are returning into my hands.
I am returning to love and life
From all the dead of all the lands.

IMPERIAL COMMAND

Tonight no one shall sleep in my nation:
One times one equals one thousand.
I was disturbed by the beckonings
That flared up from this calculation.

Like scientists we shall acquire the knowledge
Of the stars and darkness by dawn.
Is it the touch of ancient sultans:
Each book has a gilded edge?

To share in the universe and its blessing
Let everyone fill his hands with rock and soil
      and wind
Until they all turn white
Under the sacred branches of the morning.

I know beautiful things about love and death
From the emerald ponds and marble baths.
All I know is: Soon a state shall be founded
Far greater than my country's breadth.

The imperial command that I made my town
      criers shout
Is all too clear on the green of the leaves;
Let him who holds his life in faith
Break the circle drawn around him by walking out.

With its huge dark letters the sky is hard to read,
I am the sultan but I am afraid just the same.
Let everyone draw his life from me tonight,
Let everyone live in my name.

A CORPSE TURNS COLD

In the distance, the hearses came to a halt.
In a far-off temple, the candle went dead.
At midnight all the corpses turned pale,
And faith left the body as in a deathbed.

Kites were soaring dawn after dawn:
The wind snatched a kite from a kid.
Climates at their loveliest, all blue:
The tallies, like a flask, were emptied.

And songs in villages, from light and toil,
Stars swimming like fish in the northern skies,
The seas whose waves give life its form
But beyond which no ocean lies.

Far away, the pounding of a brave heart,
In infidel factories, trains full of spring.
Twinkles return to its distance
As dreams that the ultimate images bring.

Crucifixes are affirmations of eternity;
Horizons are their own lack.
It stretches into the sky as a line;
Turn the lamp off, smoke is raging black.

A mad crowd beckons and rejoices,
Thrusting in my way their hands like bony threats.
"Someone else has arrived, someone else"
O sky teeming with minarets.

Those I left behind are with me now,
The mercy, silence, and fear of hearts.
The world's wooden stairway.
In the huge barracks the guard duty starts.

Caught between the two crowds, all alone,
Homeless circles in the sky's arch.
Leaving life and death behind,
Over the fallen martyrs they march.

Memories and nights are torn asunder,
Golden streams seek to have their fate revealed.
On the children swarming like ants
Doors, huge as mountains, are sealed.

All over my face, by someone's bony fingers,
Soft soil is hurled,
Then my eyes are covered by someone else
Who is jealous of his blessed world.

NIGHT IS THE SULTAN OF ANIMALS

Night is the sultan of animals,
Night with its pitchblack down
Gives me courage like a female
When I think of my loved one.

To majestic legends
The blood of dreams opens the track.
From their starknaked mountains
Savage memories launch their attack.

We wolves and birds have thronged
The marshes at a moment of rapture.
Now the whiteness of my teeth
Gleams over love and pleasure.

MY TRANSLATORS

Night turns
Darkness into light.

      Water transforms
      The soil into green.

The hand converts
Strokes into writing.

      Science transmutes
      The sky into the earth.

The wind changes
Rocks into sculpture.

      The bird translates
      Silence into song.

Heroes transfigure
Enslavement to freedom.

FELLOW CITIZEN

Before dawn spreads its light on time
Before the mountains unfurl the earth,
If any of you wake up
I too wake up.

Wind in the fields, hubbub in the marketplace:
Living renews itself again:
If any of you get hungry,
I too get hungry.

No matter how ugly, no one should be left out,
His warmth should be spared from the chill...
If any of you love,
I too love.

MELİH CEVDET ANDAY

COPPER AGE

A raven crowed without knowing why.
Faster. On a pine tree which must wait.
Our familiar summer arrived on one wing,
Not even weary, inept and lonesome.
Let's make believe we see for the first time,
Not to upset the rule. Faster.

Thinking is half of speed.
Faster. Summer should come sooner,
Winter sooner, mid-month and the child.
Concerts and ulcers, love and government
And balding, the clock should run faster
So must death... Faster.

Death is nature's being one-eyed.
Graves should be dug round. Faster.
Dead men were rotund in the copper age.
We must call loneliness nature's timidity
And death the effort to affirm the self, oh
The fear of being forgotten. Faster.

Speed is half of nature, the other half
Is death. Which means faster.
Like summer it comes without knowing why.
We must die as if it's the first time,
Not to upset the rule. Faster.
We must stall.

Nature is half of man.
Death is all of speed. Today or tomorrow.
One might just as soon die today. Faster, better too.
You might have died yesterday.
                    -Yesterday a hot wind blew,
Remember, the kids went to the movies,
My morning tea toppled on the tablecloth.

Today and tomorrow are the same,
Either a hot wind blows or the tea topples.
Why are you looking at the kids, they might all die.
Peace and war are one.
Nature and man are the same.
Speed and death are one.

A raven crowed without knowing why.
On top of a pinetree which must wait.
Nothing matters except the laws, said somebody,
Man does not concern me, never magnify death.
Someone bewildered about summer's arrival
Asked himself if life is guilt.

SIDE BY SIDE

Right beside the tumultuous leaves of grass
They nearly touch the shadow of the sea
Just when the smell of the peaches begins
Hair-breadth close to a kiss and embrace
Under the nose of the flowing brook

This cruelty, this injustice, this torment

SEAGULL

The seagull is a capital letter
Scribbled by a little child

RAIN

The rain suddenly came down with the swallows
The swallows and the rain
Which is which

DOG

The dog
Chases the autumn morning
In a playground

ONE MOMENT

The road is lovely
As if there is no death

PIGEON

The pigeon
The applause that breaks out at the window

WINDMILL

Earth silence as birds end the morning
Resounds in both worlds together,
Like a god nourished by the sweetest waters
The trees keep ripening,
And this is a single moment resembling a seed,
Delicate, in its warmth it lies tightly buried,
Far away from itself.

Wisdom stood still in its void,
An infant on the way to a fetus,
The magic of being or ceasing to be,
In the pale likeness
Of life and death, no one can know
The beginning or the end of sagacity
Any more than the vast sea.

At the feeding time of the birds I am a
        rock's shadow,
A forest dragged down to the waterside,
A dead man, as if he never died
Has pierced the soil at one end,
Like the streets of tiny birds,
I am the mill that walks away from the wind
When birds are fed at noontide.

VERTIGO

From a sea in bloom everything will burst
One day and be a forest.
From now on what you'll see is the soft hour
Of birds on the branches where they rest.
Wait for the god who waits around:
On blood-red pines, the sun
Will claw till the great night comes on.

One day, all will be sound, such sound
As travels from star to cloud and to star from
      earthly things,
So its ellipse will spread with resounding chimes.
While you eye these rings,
Wait for the voice among voices to rebound.
Passing through organ-music, the hair-winged moon
Will come out quite soon.

I have lived in the wind.
Vertigo turned into lonely day. Alone,
My prophets were far-off rocks.
Neither forest nor sound, all by myself, windblown
Rain comforts the soul.
If not, godlike we must wait around
To hear a voice or any sound.

From ODYSSEUS BOUND

Part II, Section 5

It is neither cloud nor leaf that goes
For a color grows big like a thought.
My hand is there so I can't hold the bough.
After gazing I forgot my eyes in the sea,
For the sky slowly turns into my memory,
No sense nor sight only the stars now.
Am I whole or a fragment, who knows?
Loaded with suns I am lost and gone;
Neither the earth is lost nor the sun.

Part II, Section 6

I scampered in an array out of kilter:
As I ran my loneliness was on the rise,
I stared out of a dinotherium's eyes
At myself - what folly! - alien in space.
A seagull that had rooted out the sea
Now kept swinging it on its beak;
Latched on to a bird the wind got feathery,
Growing denser at a slow pace
The thunder shortly became the tree.

Part III, Section 3

I had never seen these hands of mine
For they used to be my trees
Should I turn off the light now and
Get up to grab hold of my trees
Are they my hands or the names
Of my hands? Right now I am also
An achromatic color, declaration;
What is early summer but the fact
Of early summer? The extraordinary
Quaintness of ordinary shapes
Is due to their revival like the soil.

Part III, Section 7

If words are motionless in the middle of the orbit
What after all is growth without movement
"This is the mythology of modern death" *
Order apart from form, shape apart from mold
Consonance on the one hand, congruence on the other
It is not existence nor death, but the other one.
The voice between sound and quiet
Conviction without knowledge, science without faith
Substance somewhere and essence somewhere else
Feeling without sensation, sentiment without sense
Poised between the real and the ideal.

*By Wallace Stevens

ON THE NOMAD SEA

I

You and I, and our flowerpot on the balcony:
Busybee Elizabeth. The building's first triangle.

Neither old nor new. As if the most lucid
Moment of our destiny is trembling

On the nomad sea. We're not aware of it.
The sound of the rock resembles the human voice.

At a glimpse you find out: The flowerpot
On the balcony has replaced the cloud. The clouds

Turn themselves into horses in all that foam.
You and I keep running, ahead of us

A red bird shakes the ancient elder tree
A blind child was looking at a moment ago.

Then the cloud turns into the flowerpot again,
Horses begin to heave, we rest, in our ears

A murmur lingers like indecipherable words
Spoken by the walls. Out of this day, this morning.

II

Not to remember, not to forget. Where the ends meet,
Along the crimson smells of the shores,

Growing like the trills of a crippled nightingale,
In the heavy and slow symbols of our gaze.

And I emigrate to you moment by moment
I return, in an exodus, like a vibration,

Seeking the rocks of your lips,
Seeking your name which I wrote in rain.

Now you vanish in the crevices of your own valley,
Now you gush out

All over your vanished valley.
Time and again I am lost to myself.

This is all there is to it. Neither old nor new.
Like the most lucid moment of our destiny.

Countless blue transforming into a thought
Unused as those words which cannot exist alone,

Which emerge out of nowhere;
The soul is a coal crystal, rises out of darkness

Like a scarlet moon, and watches over the night.
And pioneering the numerical shapes,

It closes in on all things that scatter
And come together, like a carnivorous plant.

Scattering is none other than coming together.
The sexual fluid that breaks out of its shell,

The sun's taut, then loosened, bow, first images
Of the starry oysters twinkling.

The sky's wing turning red and growing pale;
All sorts of fruit on branches, feet sealed,

Sprouting frantically to a new infinity, then falling;
The soil whose panting like a sea lion

Moves us deep down, full of bleached bones.
Neither old nor new. That's all there is to it.

That is all. You and I and our flowerpot on
        the balcony.
Alone in the fluttering of heavy symbols.

III

There. I sprinkle all the words by the handfuls
To the birds, to the roots of roses,

To the lip of the sun, to the skirt
Of the prancing morning, to the red velvet of rocks,

To the moon's horns, and to the honeysuckle
Hanging out of the railings of your hair...

All by myself I cast my image over all shapes
And over the cross-eyed bottoms of the seas.

IV

Henry Moore is busy picking up pebbles
        on the beach,
Little fertile, some with holes in the middle,

Just like women's teats, like figs,
Dreams on their shoulders.

The heart is meant for the wisdom that no form
Is doomed to suffering.

Rocks that ennoble the world, with lodes,
        slab by slab,
Wave like flags that have wiped

The blood stains of being alive.
Bones, all those human bones and animal bones,

The daintiest and the mightiest wreaths
Of the passage from one shape to another.

And the sea shells, grooved inside out,
Smell of shadows like the forehead of a billy goat.

Delight was meant to cross
Animals and grass.

All those trunks of trees covered
With graffiti like the walls of the mad...

The locked gem of the birds
Transforming the dead into the stars.

Man craved more, so much more.
All the more. Neither old nor new.

Perhaps it is a giant that dies and is resurrected
Time and again or a goddess frightened to death

These mute monuments which bloom like flowers
With their helter-skelter lines to the eye.

The eye is the god of its own harmony,
Segment by segment, against and opposite the whole.

Shape turning into shape, the resounding water
Of the present, life's alarm clock;

The enigmatic masts of change, the shriek,
The diamond of action, woman, noun and verb.

Like a bull that dashes through a village
I shood away whatever you had in you.

Now I know how hard it is to divest oneself
Of a two-dimensional raid and to live in a
        blue moment.

If the eye that sees is the eye that is seen
Then I am someone else.

This framework belongs neither to yesterday
        nor to tomorrow.
Tomorrow is an image, so is yesterday.

The sea, the bird, the wind, the rain
Belong to this day, this morning.

V

Freud is seated in the subconscious of a tree,
He keeps poking the dreams of the earth.

There are poppies that brighten these dreams.
Sea, bird, wind, rain.

The dream, a star distilled late
From action's bed of milky figs,

Late or early, the fish that leaps suddenly
Out of yesterday's waters;

A scarlet turmoil that has turned daylight inside out,
The face of a cramped well asleep and awake.

Epochs seem hidden in seeds,
Swings creaking in the soil.

Sea, bird, rain, wind.
And I found myself crucified

Between the past and the future, like a dream.
Neither old nor new. As if the most lucid

Moment of our destiny is trembling
In the waters of the sea laid waste.

İLHAN BERK

I WOKE, THIS MEANT A LOVE IN THE WORLD

I woke, this meant a love in the world
- Your voice was like forsaking a rose.
I was black, like paper on all sorts of life
Each day my name was on those seas could you see
For a millennium I was an M sound in Lower Egypt.

I beat down on loves didn't anyone notice
For a millennium I unfurled you in my loneliness.
Whenever my name came up in your bright light
This meant a love in the world.

In Egypt once upon a time solitude was lovely
That was a brave new sky one could cross with you
When I glanced it grew like a lily in my memory
Now it's a shadow that grows tall in my meadows
This is the way I woke which wasn't really waking
This meant a love in the world.

FOR HOMER

I

Homer led a tranquil life. Like mountain roads.
Quietly he prepared himself - the way
water is ready to flow -
for the principles of poetry.

Like all the great poets of the world
he studied bird and beast, the raging sea
and the first flames and flashes of the day.

That is why Homer resembles Homer alone.

II

We know Homer as the master of long poems
And long suffering.
              Thus on this globe
His long robe and high stature went and came back.

METROPOLIS

In the house of the sea I saw you. You were as pretty as an afternoon. A fish kept changing waters. Every day we climbed the brand new walls of depression. Your name intruded upon our boredom. As growth was stepped up, you increased.

"The sky can be heard," I said.

I arrived in oppression's quiet realm

I am walking you.

"NEVER DID I SEE SUCH LOVES NOR SUCH SEPARATIONS"

Whenever I think of you
A gazelle goes down to drink water
And I see the meadows expanding

With you each evening
One green olive
And a piece of the blue sea
Take me along

Each time I dream of you
I plant roses where my hand touches
I give water to the horses
And I love the mountains even more

WOMEN

They stand there and chat near the breakwater,
Their voices force the birds to take flight,
　　　leaves to shed.
Women of who knows which eras.

There are times when the world comes to a standstill
Some day together we had pressed flowers to dry
In a notebook:
　　　　　Women are something like that
Who knows when, where, suddenly,
It turns out we have lived a voice
　　　　　　　　　they have left with us.

CAHİT KÜLEBİ

A STORY OF THE SEA

We shall always swim together in these blue waters
In this vervain sea that resembles your face.
Beating together, both my pulse and yours
Will strike at death and denounce darkness.

All the fish will chase us from the depths,
Saying Külebi is here now with his loved one.
Like a gull swooping from the vast horizon
The wind will drop shafts of light like pearls.

And the pearls will glitter around your neck,
On your chest and arms, like the words of my verses,
Sea anemone on your hair, your most secret parts,
Like rain, the stars will glide in your eyes.

Our love shall make these blue flames sacred.

DURING THE WAR

Each night fathers came home ashamed
During the war
Mothers' breasts were drained of milk
And the babies cried.
Men went to war.
Women stayed behind like skeletons.
Young girls grew pale during the war.

And from all those battles
Nothing remains but a memory.

OFFICIAL LEAVE

If I can get official leave and come
You'll laugh, you'll be so happy.
We shall rise early in the morning
And get the stove going.
The tint of my tobacco will make your hair lovely,
Your hands will smell of tea,
Your voice will give rise to dawn.

LIVING

I

In the dungeon of seasons
Tall iron bars stand,
In the dungeon of desires
She untangles her braid.

In the dungeon of gardens
All the flowers are untended,
In the dungeon of clouds
A white archipelago floats.

In the dungeon of nights
This poet languishes alone,
In the dungeon of hopes
Neither a soul stirs nor a ghoul.

II

What makes me a captive to the world,
Why is it me, I want to know?
I have feet and I want to walk,
I have teeth and I want to laugh,
I have eyes and I want to sleep.

O God, I want to know
Is your place in heaven above our land?

SALAH BİRSEL

GEOGRAPHY LESSON

The subject of today's lesson is geography
Don't be wary at all to go near the guys
There Bolu forests are straight ahead
Take a love stroll early in the morning
Don't be bashful our subject is geography

Look this is the place they call Asia
Here's Beyoğlu Avenue this is in Hong Kong
Watch your step don't crush the Chinese
Stuff the yellowest of them into your bag
Don't forget our subject is geography

I could tell this was going to happen
See you smashed the Calcutta elephants
Hold it now climb the Himalayas at least
Take off your clothes at the Tibet plateau
Don't be shy our subject is geography

- Bolu: a mountainous province of Turkey

Miss you aren't listening to our lecture
Look these are the sultans of Africa
Who tirelessly eat pineapple four seasons
Well love your Ethiopian lads if you like
Don't be ashamed our subject is geography

And these here are the Alps
Don't say you can't see for all those men
Going down you have the Venetian counts
Go to sleep in the streets of Rome at noon
Don't forget our subject is geography

Now look this is the sea of Paris
Held in the hand of Queen Brigitte Bardot
And higher up you have the Bank of England
High time you made off with the sterlings
Don't be scared our subject is geography

That's all for today some other time
We'll see the United States with Texas Rangers
But go ahead hug your husbands right away
I guess your husbands won't mind it either
Don't forget our subject is geography

POETRY LESSON

Take "Love for mankind" as your topic
And free verse as prosody,
Relevant or not,
Whenever it occurs to you,
Insert the word "Hunger"
At a convenient spot.
Near the end of the poem
Rhyme "strife" with "the right to good life."

There - that's the way to become A Great Poet.

INVITATION TO SLOTH

Hold it gentlemen relax for a while
Why are we in this maddening rat race
Straining our hearts for what
Instead let's develop double chins
And sit back and relax for a while

Whoever wants to stand or stalk let him
But let's squat right here on the ground
First let's open our mouths wide
Then stretch and relax our shoulders
And even roll over our eyes
Gentlemen let's yawn for a while

Who cares if we make a couple of bucks
Instead let's contemplate our navel
Turn a cold shoulder to work and thought
Or else no one would sympathize with us
While there's still time kids and grown-ups
Let's doze off let's live in sloth
Gentlemen let's snore for a while

SABAHATTİN KUDRET AKSAL

CROWS

I

It's the crow that keeps his loneliness alive
On the asphalt
All by himself

II

He's reticent
Because he's mortal
But he keeps talking
Because he's mortal

III

The weight of a crow
Is the sum of my weight
One night till daybreak

IV

A sun pitch-black like his feathers
Warms his up
Rainy glittering

V

He flies from my sleep
To my wakefulness

VI

Crows are the choicest flowers
Of my eyes

VII

Diverse like all nights
Like all orphans

VIII

And on a very long line
Keeps going back and forth

IX

The crow that rings the night's doorbell
Will draw circles of light
In the dark

X

Why are you looking at me
With your eyes fixed on me
One light isn't similar to another

XI

Going round and round in the room
Hitting against walls and ceilings
In a hue and cry

XII

All night
Medieval crows in my dream

XIII

A sun-drenched street
When you happen to look
Might not be bright

XIV

A morning without crows
Geometric

XV

Out of the tiny window of those huge towers
Clouds of crows break loose

SPEAKING

I was speaking and speaking and speaking,
Right next to you; the sun covered with weed in the
        ancient language
Of constellations. I turned quiet, you woke in
        my silence!

CLOUD

Where a cloud blossoms
Death is not relevant!

POETRY

I am silent. As soon as I turn silent I feel that it
        begins poetry.
Right beside me, that shadow without shadows keeps
        waiting to speak.

NECATİ CUMALI

MOZART'S BIRDS

The clock strikes nine
He will spend the morning at the piano
As sparrows cheerfully chirp outside
Skipping from this branch to that
With his eyes on the light-filled window
When his fingers coddle the keys
A little sonata by Mozart begins
Sparrows break into silence
The light glittering on the walls
Are all Mozart's now
And the birds that chirp in the glare
Are Mozart's birds

For two years each morning this little sonata
Each morning with a new meaning
Like life itself ceaselessly glowing and gleaning
A life better and nicer and more real
Casts aside our obscure abstruse speech
And we listen to ourselves like water and leaves

Weary of obsession and worry
To believe and to hope anew
Not free of the heart's swift disillusion
In the night's silence
Or in distant meadows in the morning
To find and to lose Mozart

SUN CRAZE

I love the flowing waters
I adore the gleaming snow
A green leaf
A forked insect
A sprouting seed
Fill my heart with joy
When I see them in the sun

A day
A lovely day
A sunny day
I wouldn't give up for anything
That's why I abhor war
And brutality

I know they cannot survive in the sun
Or in the aura of love
Injustice
Fear
Hunger

A FEAR AMONG FEARS

For three days I looked forward to Sunday
Till Sunday you had said
Believe me for three days
I longed for nothing but Sunday
Could neither sleep nor work well
Till Sunday I said and waited

Sunday morning
A fear among fears
Played havoc with my joy
What if you are not the one I love
What if you are not the one I crave

AT THE INQUEST

-- At Urla's Özbek Village, Orphan Ali shot his
neighbor Slim Ömer for trespassing one-sixteenth of an
acre into his land. Let us now hear what the Özbek
villagers and the wives of Ali and Ömer had to say
about the incident and what testimonies they gave at
the gendarme station.

I

Ballad of a Villager who saw Ömer at dawn on the
Morning of the Shooting

At that daybreak hour
I saw Ömer on his auburn horse
Galloping from down there
He had his hunter's jacket on
And leather boots on his feet

Dewdrops twinkled on the grass
Flanked by poplars green and white
A bird dashed ahead of him
And the brook beckoned from behind
While Özbek lay in dense shadows

Fresh blues bloomed into the sky
At that daybreak hour
Ömer rode his auburn horse
Greeted the flying bird and the newborn day
I saw him coming from down there

II

The Elegy of the Old Women of Özbek

This morning at Özbek
We ran out at gunfire
This morning at Özbek
Windows were opened to gunfire
A tearful daylight flooded our homes
And the downcast skies
Dangled before our eyes

Go take a good look
Where gunfire can't be heard
Are the white-plastered roofs
Brooks flowing white
And the white poplars over there
As black and grim as this?

Go take a good look
Where people are in love
See the sun there
See the sky
See the soil
Joyful and happy

Then come take a look at us
See how the sky flies away from us
Our children shudder when we pat them
Fear reigns in our hearts
Our brides are pale as withering saplings

III

The First Elegy of Killer Ali's Wife

For three days, three long days
Since Ömer's plough cut into our land
Tuesday Wednesday and Thursday
For three days, three long days
My Ali grew dark and grim with fury
Not a trace of a smile on his face

Tuesday Wednesday and Thursday
Morning noon and evening
I set a useless table for him
His head sagging
My Ali didn't even touch the bread

Three nights, three long nights went by
His eyes fixed on the ceiling beams
He smoked one cigarette after another,
Deep in thought and with deeper sighs
These three nights of my life
My Ali didn't embrace me or caress me

Three days and three nights went by
Tuesday Wednesday and Thursday
His heart was scorched
When his eyes caught a glimpse
Of our son or daughter or me
He plunged into deep thoughts
My Ali my brave Ali

IV

The Second Elegy of Ali's Wife

Ominous evil darkness
Hovered over our house
My heart in anguish
Tortured by fear and worry
I clutched his hands:
"Don't, Ali dear, don't!"

Ominous evil silence
Roamed about our house
Then I saw Ali get up
His revolver on his hip
I stood before him:
"Don't go, Ali dear, don't!"

I looked him straight in the eye
I'd never seen him like that
He'd never hurt a bird or ant
My arms dropped my strength ebbed
I fell at his feet and stayed there
Then I felt the chill through the door
And heard the three shots

V

The Elegy of the Dead Man's Wife

A brook flows past our house
Flanked by three poplars
All planted by my Ömer
It was Ömer who broke ground
For the foothpath down to the brook
In our front yard my Ömer raised
Geraniums and mint and dandelions

Year in year out
If our hearth was on and we had gas
And my Ömer beamed with a smile
The poplars rejoiced too
But if my Ömer was downhearted
When the crop was poor and flour scarce
Then the poplar turned dark too

Year in year out
When I got home his breath fondled my face
At night if we went out into the front yard
Geraniums and mint and dandelions smelled so nice

I can no longer look at the path to our brook
Nor at the white poplars
Out of the windows or through the doorway
I can no longer look at the sun or at the moon
Now whenever I come home my heart aches
The smell of geraniums and mint and dandelions
Out in the front yard
Is like a curse on me!

VI

The Elegy of the Old Men of Özbek Village

At Özbek's Akkum site
Flanked by mountains
Sea to the West, brook to the South
A stony cragged chalky field
Runs between the mountain and the sea
A stunted wild pear tree in the middle
Cuts the field into two or does it
Ali tills the Northern part
From the mountain to the tree
Ömer tills the South from the tree to the brook

Hey there, poor Ali, for shame
Hey there, poor Ömer, for shame

One day we saw Ömer's plough
One-sixteenth of an acre past the tree
For as long as we can recall
South was Ömer's up to the tree
And the Northern part was Ali's

Hey there, poor Ali, for shame
Hey there, poor Ömer, for shame

At Özbek's Akkum site
Between the mountain and the sea
A stony cragged chalky field
A couple of skimpy olive trees
A couple of stunted wild pear trees
Scorched under the sun
Green under the rain
Couch grass and jackal weed and thistle

Hey there, poor Ömer, for shame
Hey there, poor Ali, for shame

We saw the sun on the pear trees and
        the olive trees
As a cool breeze blew from the mountain
The sea stirred with mad blue foam
We saw the couch grass turn green
While others wilted
We saw
Ant hills standing still
And locusts
And solomon's seals stood still
We looked
No more does Ali show up
Nor is there any sight of Ömer

Hey there, poor Ömer, for shame
Hey there, Poor Ali, for shame

ATTİLA İLHAN

THE DEAD GROW OLD

the downpour of stars is no less than a servile salute
lilies are white and whites are no less than lilies
over the marshes mosquitoes multiply by the million
bugs and insects are linked forever in hug and embrace
the downpour of stars is no less than a servile salute

all the old equestrians hoof the wayworn up the hill
sweltering in galaxies horses will burst inside out
on hoary battlefields lie the wounded and the martyred
pines and willows are linked forever in hug
        and embrace
should a girl come alive or a mortal die or a star fall
all the old equestrians hoof the wayworn up the hill

hyenas refuse to recall the saturnalia and all
life's flight from the body and man's from humanity
a hundred killed a hundred orphaned a hundred lost
mothers raise their sons for combat overseas
hyenas refuse to recall the saturnalia and all
should a girl come alive or a mortal die or a star fall
whoever is dead is dead and the dead have grown old.

ANCIENT SEA FOLK

pebbles chant an odd song there and the sea
      shepherds
drive their herds into the high seas
while on the mussels' iris harlot blues crouch
in the boundless western time's green galleons
unforgettable and emerald and sighted
blood-drenched slab by slab
you hear the ancient sea folk in harbor taverns
those kinky sea people if you listen
spanish songs and italian wine
and god-like you create curses
from 15 meridian to 20 you create universal curses
atop the mainmast
you god of blasphemy and tumult and of my enigma
you god of lost treasures
you shall not look behind nor spit at the wind
unless black flags are hoisted on the admiral's mast
no honest breeze shall spark your corsair's eyes
unless you chew on the rain or on tobacco

I never forgot the mediterranean
I plunged into flames and wept voraciously
the joy of creating
and being created flared tremulously in the sky
and prayers burst open like titanic sails
then lo and behold three crescents arose at once
barbarossa songs released like hawks from their arms
cyclone-sized barefoot mariners of the algerian skipper
who arrested the caravans of ships   ./..

and held the straits of messina and septe and all others
there is no god but God
arrested and set all the vessels on fire
fire's joyous and memorable dominion
stirs in constellations and beacons isthmus by isthmus
then bound for rome in legion with hannibal
the phoenicians carried the alphabet and the glass
        long ago
dragons breathed fire and the avatars of the
        sea monsters
and the ghost of a genoese galley slave haunted a
        rhodes castle
his feet shackled
a dagger stuck in his back
while latin songs poured forth
from the vessels of antonius

you unexpected unforgettable unbearable and deep
        and magnified
as roguish as a cabin-boy or a sailor's moustache
the wind uncontained in its rose and in its own
        dimensions
the centuries-old buccaneer fate of yours
tattooed on your arms and infinitely on your chest
green and speckled
angelface mermaids and unctuous dolphins
you sense from the world what the children sense
while time keeps aging you remain a child
you are the ancient sea cemetery of pirates and sailors ./..

the graveyard of barbarossa songs
with your mighty waves you are the ocean
the starry multitudes of the plankton and the skate
you are god and bear gods in your kingdom
the master skippers who tyrannize the currents
        and eddies
cruise north-northeast and some cruise westward
there once was a captain joy whom we buried in
        the iceberg sea
an andersen and a kid
a salih a burak and a memi
together exploding our laughter as canons in salvo
at a giants' carnival
winnowed and scattered we had died
then the fish-garths near the shores and archipelagos
being so ancient and stately as to defy memory
forsaking all the stars to recognize the north star
        at one glance
italian fishermen with beards dripping with salt
then as in purgatory ravelled and fibrous
to disembark sahara-parched at a port where foxes
        spit copper
and to come abroad truculent in a deluge of wine
blessed be thy name
whenever we cruise towards the south pole
from tierra del fuego
from the flameland

- "Barbarossa" Hayreddin Pasha was the Admiral of the
  Ottoman Fleet at the time of Süleyman the
  Magnificent (16th Century); Salih and Burak were also
  legendary naval commanders.

ARİF DAMAR

OFFERING

Does one wait for lovely days to enjoy them
Waiting itself. is lovely too

THAT'S BLOOD THERE...

Blood of honor blood daunted blood and how
There's no morning sleep without moonbeams
            blood suppressed blood exhausted
Blood on iron cement wire which we avoid and
            pretend not to notice
Ill at ease dishevelled passionate blood
Blood half dead in the rose and in whisky
Getting thinner spending itself dying up
On fingernails and in the tears

AHMET ARİF

THIRTY-THREE BULLETS

I

This mountain is Mt Mengene
When dawn breaks open over Van
This mountain is Nimrod's child
When dawn breaks open across from Nimrod's mountain
On one side, the Caucasian horizon, avalanches grow
On your other side, the prayer rug is Persia
Glaciers on the peaks are like bunches of fruit
Fugitive pigeons stand at waterside
And a herd of deer
And a flock of partridges...

No one can deny their heroism
They were undefeated in one-on-one combat
The loyal sons of this region for millennia
How are we going to break the news now
This is not a flock of cranes
Nor a constellation up in the sky
This is a heart pierced by thirty-three bullets
Thirty-three fountains of blood
No longer flowing,
Now a lake on this mountain...

II

A rabbit jumped up from the bottom of the hill
Its back is speckled
Its belly white as milk
Poor thing is a pregnant mountain hare
Its heart leaps to its mouth
Seeing it any man can give up hunting
It was a desolate hour a lonely time
A spotless, starknaked dawn
One of the thirty-three looked
Hunger's void weighed down on his stomach
His long hair and beard were messed up
Lice crawled on his collar
He saw that he had been shot in the arms
A hero with an infernal heart
Looked first at the pitiful hare
Then looked back there.

Suddenly his dainty carbine came to his mind
Sullen under his pillow,
Then he thought of the colt he had brought from the
        Harran plains
The colt's mane had blue beads,
His forehead had a blaze,
Three of his fetlocks were white
His cantering generous and brisk
With the chestnut mare
How the two of them had taken flight
        in front of Hozat!
If he weren't helpless and tied down like this,
If there were no cold barrel of a gun propped
        in his back,
He might have hidden up on the heights.
These friendly mountains know a man's worth,
And Heaven knows, these hands will never bring shame,
These hands can masterfully fell with the first shot
The ash of the burning cigarette
Or the viper's forked tongue
Sparkling in the sun...

These eyes which had never been duped, not even once,
Knew full well the doomsday of the passes waiting for
        an avalanche
And the soft snowy treachery
Of the cliffs...
There was no escape
He was going to get shot
Final orders had been issued:
Blind reptiles were to gobble up his eyes
And vultures his heart.

III

I got shot
In a desolate mountain pass
At the time of the morning prayer
I'm lying here
Stretched out, drenched in blood...

I got shot
My dreams are darker than the nights
I try to find a good omen but it's no use
They have taken my life before my time was up
It would take volumes to tell my story
A pasha sends an order in code
And I get shot without due process, without an inquest.

Brother, write all about my plight word for word
Lest others think it might be hearsay
What I have in my shattered mouth
Are not rosy teats
But dumdum bullets...

IV

They executed the orders to kill.
They dipped in blood
The blue haze of the mountain
And the half-asleep breeze of dawn.
Then they stacked their guns
Slowly they frisked our bodies.
They turned my crimson sash
Of Kirmanshah weave inside out,
They went away taking with them
My rosary and my cigarette case
Which were gifts from Persia...

We are kith and kin, blood relations
For centuries we have exchanged brides
With the villages and nomads on the other side
We are neighbors, kissing cousins
Our hens mingle together
All this not because we don't know any better
But because of poverty,
We have never warmed up to passports
This is the crime that has caused them to murder us
We have been branded
Smugglers
Highwaymen
Traitors...

Brother, write all about my plight word for word
Lest others think it might be hearsay
What I have in my shattered mouth
Are not rosy teats
But dumdum bullets...

V

Shoot, bastards
Shoot all you want,
I won't die so easily,
My embers are alive in the ashes,
I still have a lot to say in my guts
To those who'll get my meaning.
My father lost his eyes on the Urfa front
And his three brothers
Who were like three slender cypresses,
Three hunks of mountain still yearning to live.
That's when our kith and kin, the sons of the tribe
Were fighting the bullets of the French
From fortresses, hills and minarets.

My younger uncle Nazif
His moustache barely out yet
Handsome
Light-footed
Good horseman
He said: "Shoot, brother
"Shoot:
"This is the day to defend our honor!"
And reared his horse on its hind legs...

Brother, write all about my plight word for word
Lest others think it might be hearsay
What I have in my shattered mouth
Are not rosy teats
But dumdum bullets...

CAN YÜCEL

HISTORY LESSON AT THE FLEA MARKET

If you recline into this brocaded couch
And if I go sit on that shelf of turbans
Do you think we might upset the venerable dust?
If we take a pinch out of this snuffbox,
Which probably belonged to some Grand Mufti,
Do you think it might drum up a sneeze,
The parable of the snuff long since gone?

Is this the end of the auction or just about?
After all, no more bids are to be heard.
Before the gavel sounded to announce Mr. N.
The owner of a full-length gold-leaf mirror
And before he could even say, "It's all done,"
Before his new piece jibed with the new features,
Mr. N., his mirror, his comb and his auburn locks
All turned to dust and were scattered to the wind.
Is this the end of the auction or just about?

Were you ever, while sitting at a train window,
By the drifting trees and the earth and the rocks,
Deep in thought, watching the images of your face
With the twitches on your mouth and what not,
Jabbed and jostled by the rude elbow
Of some guy breezing through the corridor?

Did you then wish you were the only passenger?
Dismissing all that you wistfully watched --
The trees, the earth, the rocks and yourself
Out of the window of the speeding train,
Did you wish you were left behind there
Where you had seen your image reflected?

Surely you have wished for that, haven't we all?

How about me buying you a mirror,
A full-length mirror with a gold-leaf frame
With the inscription on top "Here lies the deceased"?
And then we'll have your body washed clean
And in your memory we'll send out trays of fritters.

Surely you have wished for that, haven't we all?

Mr. N. had the urge to get off before
        the train stopped.
Yet these are venerable secondhand mirrors
And venerable mirrors fall into disuse,
With dust upon dust, and dust inside dust,
Venerable mirrors have fallen into disuse.

No one may get off while the train is moving.
If you do, they won't wash you the right way,
But they'll bury you at the Flea Market
        before you rot.

Surely you have wished for that, haven't we all?

Whatever remains after you are gone
Or whatever has remained after Mr. N. was gone
In a handful of dust,
Was it the unlived portion of his life?
Or whatever has remained after Mr. N. was gone
In a handful of dust,
Was it his death in defiance of dying?

They won't let you get off while the train is moving;
If you do, they won't wash you the right way,
They'll bury you at the Flea Market before you rot.

They won't allow you to mellow like wine
Or become an old man in the shade of a plane tree;
You shall remain idle in the midst of the mirrors
With dust upon dust, a passenger on the train,
Neither within the entrance nor without,
A Flea Market shopper with Flea Market items
      for sale.
If you live, you shall live with the dead at best,
Neither within the entrance nor without,
If you die, you shall die with death itself.

If you recline into this brocaded couch
And if I go sit on that shelf of turbans
Do you think we might upset the venerable dust?
If we take a pinch out of this snuffbox,
Which probably belonged to some Grand Mufti,
Do you think it might drum up a sneeze,
The parable of the snuff long since gone?

HERETIC

Mosques could do without minarets
Our world could revolve without God
So long as you have a loudspeaker there

POEM SIX

I had said: I want to live living,
And yet now on this roof willy-nilly
My feet and my rhymes are fettered,
My days pass with such lame feet of verse,
Don't think I'm bragging if I say so myself,
My life is my loveliest poem.

POEM TWENTY-SIX

We have two kinds of people who know the subtleties
       of politics
Politicians and convicts.
The reason is obvious:
For politicians, politics is the danger of getting thrown
       into jail,
For convicts, it is the prospect of getting out.

JUST LIKE THAT...

I put on my clean shirt after the drill,
Soldiers washed their feet at the fountain;
Yours was a coolness just like that.
As we rode in station wagons down to the city
It was wonderful to call the nude a "civilian"
And out of the day-open window of the oak trees
The blue took shelter in the hill's shady slope,
And you were a tiny portion of the sea.

The emigrant sun of Albanian villages
Settled on school windows with sharp spices;
And you were a Saturday just like that.
Girls combed their hair on the train's vestibule,
That's why the rails shoot off sparks like this.
As they turn the corners, from under their aprons
The odor of their period dawns upon the world;
You were the red trolley that took off from
        my early youth.

By the fruit market at a coffeehouse for
        the early birds
Though daylight was yet to break, I said
        "Good morning."
You were a bright spot beaming just like that.
I never knew there was a bakery here at all;
Kneeling on the asphalt pavement, I looked down,
        oooh, oooh!
Bakers and flames and the smell of fresh bread;
Faced with solitudes I was no longer alone.
I made a mad dash and ran down the slope.
If life is a wedding, then you are the bride there.
I stripped you naked, Güler, and I donned the world.

CEMAL SÜREYA

KISS ME THEN GIVE BIRTH TO ME

Now
it is shame that becomes the grains
in the blond children's ears of corn.

From the meadow
a blindfolded lilac smell from the meadow
spins around that tiny sun of ours.

Overflowing from houses and terraces
it comes and settles in my voice.

My voice's bending hemlock
my voice's motley hemlock.

And towards the birds
the ivory: the wind's stance.
Mountain: the sun's skeleton.

Among wooden statues
The sea's baby is huge.

I see blood I see rock
among all the statues
the nightmare warm and greenhorn
--insomnia's milky fig--
does not penetrate the beehives.

My mother died when I was very young
kiss me, then give birth to me.

THE 8:10 FERRY

You know what there is in your voice?
There is the core of a garden
          Blue silk winter flower.
          You go on the upper deck
          To smoke a cigarette

                    -

You know what there is in your voice?
There is our sleepless Turkish language.
          You don't care for your job
          You dislike this city
          A man is folding his newspaper

                    -

You know what there is in your voice?
There's kissing as in olden days
          The icy bathroom window
          You failed to show up for a few days
          There are school songs

                    -

You know what there is in your voice?
There's the untidiness of a house
          Every now and then you lift your hand
          Up to your forehead and smooth out
          Your wind-swept loneliness

                    -

You know what there is in your voice?
There are words you haven't spoken
          Trivial things perhaps
          But at this time of day
          They stand like monuments

You know what there really is in your voice?
There are words you haven't been able to speak.

ROSE

Seated at the core of the rose I weep
As I die in the street each night
Ahead and beyond all unmindful
Pang upon pang of dark diminution
Of eyes upheld blissful with life

Your hands are in my caress into dusk
Hands forever white forever white
Cast into my soul icicles of fright
A train a while at the station
A man who lost the station me

On my face I rub the rose
Fallen forlorn over the pavement
And cut my body limb by limb
Bloodgush doomsday madmusic
On the horn a gypsy is reborn

YELLOW BLIGHT

My breath is a red bird
In the auburn skies of your hair
When I embrace you
Your legs grow long beyond words

My breath becomes a red horse
I can tell from my burning cheeks
We are destitute, our nights are snort
Let's make love at full tilt

JUST AT THESE HOURS

Just at these hours the water bleeds like a fresh wound
At the ends of streets, at their tiny tips.
Your eyes -- the cistern of the sun --
Are like an object that should not be in a house
Mourning the dead, like a shattered mirror.
At these hours.
Here we watch a man carrying a ladder
Like Christ who is never seen without his crucifix
We see a man carrying twelve steps on his back
I love him so much, and this bird too
You share this love; anyway, when you love
You weed out the whole earth
As the trellises hanging over the mouths of
        the buildings
Go way beyond their own boundaries,
Dogs bark up a secret mountain.

These are good I say these know all about you
Or else how could the fish
That live on the border of carbon
Know of the day of exodus leaking out of the bucket
How could the Moslems enamored of miracles
Hang their overcoats on the Prophet's fingers
And enter God's house?
And how could the mountain roads
Near which the Greeks copulated with goats
During the Return of the Ten Thousand be decked out?

And yet and yet each word we use
While making love
Is the furniture knocked over by a burglar.

Streets turned violet with minibuses
Where they trade wheat for money
Trade money with bread
Trade bread with tobacco
Trade tobacco with suffering
And where suffering is not bartered for anything any more
In those streets.
The clocks show the rain,
Today, this tiny Tuesday
Istanbul lacks everything except its hills.
Only Galata
Galata
Slowly feeds to the sea
Its inexhaustible passion for rusting
That it nurtured in the night's basements
In the form of a harmonica

Our roots flinch from their own flowers

TALAT SAİT HALMAN

A LAST LULLABY

The only morbid thing my mother did
was to let an orange rot on the porch.
I doubt if it was a symbol for her:
she did not see the molds as cruel fate,
the flies as hubris, the smell as despair.
She would gaze at it and whisper to it
the way she had once sung her lullabies.
"May be," said my brother, "she hopes to turn
it into a fruit of paradise." No - -
all she wanted was to stare and murmur:
and the orange just stared back and murmured.
They lulled each other to one last remorse.

ECE AYHAN

MASTER'S WORK

I

The destitute bird never forgets, it was the year of
    book burnings

We saw the stately entrance through forty gates
Of a headless horse and its rider with faded
    ornaments

Dervishes said shattered death was returning
    from the east

That is why a city is divided into three by a
    brackish stream

II

The destitute bird never forgets, boys whose
    masters are dead
Combed each other's hair when they came
    out of the sea

Oh Istanbul my wild lad the choicest slice of
    the watermelon
Embarrassed you hide your heart and smell like
    rotten flowers

Above a reading-selection city black pigeons are flying

III

The destitute bird never forgets the golden
         dialectical law
In history so many princes have thus carried their
         horses without knowing it

See on their sarcophagi are carved odes which are the
         master's work.

MONUMENT OF THE UNKNOWN STUDENT

Look here, underneath this black marble
Is buried a child who would have come
         to the blackboard
From nature if he had one more breath of life
He was killed in the class on Government

The wrong question posed by both government and
         nature was:
"Where does Transoxiana run into?"
The only correct answer from a hand raised in the
         last row was:
"Into the heart of the rebellion of pale
         lowerclass children."

To suppress this death, too, his old father,
         secondhand peddler,
Who tied around his neck a purple embroidered
         kerchief, wrote:
I mean I had convinced him that he had his toys.

Since that day his mother, washerwoman at night,
    who wears
A soldier's wintercoat and secretly suckles the foal
    of deer, dictated:
Oh they put my son's hard work in his hands.

His friends wove this poem out of oleanders:
Don't worry, No. 1281 at the tuition-free NCO
    school of suicide,
In every child's heart there is an older child
On children's holidays the whole class will send you
    birds not tucked into envelopes.

CEVAT ÇAPAN

THE STEPPE

It's the sea we've longed for, the sea
with its tide
the white gulls
flying about on gray days,
in an immense silence
heading for the night
bright and warm
we've longed for the sea.

SENTIMENTAL EDUCATION

The ringdove keeps thinking and brooding
Perched on the vicious cycle of underdevelopment,
Who knows in which phase of Westernization,
It takes refuge in the dead end of nausea and
                                        depression.

Drowning its passion every night in cloudy booze,
It fails to fly over the ramparts of Byzantium;
Groping through the darkness that grows dense in its
                                        heart,
It aspires to be like the poets in whose lines deer
                                        wander about.

AHMET OKTAY

ALL MEN DIE

Because the skies grow white with boredom
the wind wrinkles and the leaf falls
and in the midst of a withered blue
the gulls escape and the crimson deer.
There, see the gold and black currents
mothers, lost souvenir picture
poverty, that frightful woman.
Quiet, it's the day for all remembrance,
black rain and the rainbow
Slowly gently all men die.

Human voices should stand still
For trucks may fall off the mountain road.
A silver watch in hock at the pawnbroker
and the suitcase forgotten at the checkroom
are meteors that come to pass
through the air and the blue celluloid.
Loneliness with its defective marble
is a sacred prey offered to God,
then it turns into the lustre of ruby.

Because the skies grow white with blood
a vein throbbing and out of breath
in the heart of the petulant sea
and in the pulse of the soil,
bloodstream is like being forgotten.
The gallows and the cross and the flower
shiver in the same wind,
the whisper of the bed should cease,
the amber glittering in the hand:
with bread, shackled and heads bowed,
the men of those women pass by.
And the sad delta of brief lives
an album, a song, a child.

The ruby of some frozen sorrow
as pale as the scratch pads of kids
sparkles over the battlefields,
all the groves are the moonlight,
loves are the fulcrum you cannot reach,
the dirge that slashes and makes the
            hands bleed.
Oblivion is what lingers in the mind,
Leaping, defeated, dying deer
pen and pencil from which agony never strays.
Men are a brief word,
"No pasaran" in Spain,
church bells turning red
a long shadow over the cathedrals
"Mamma mia" in Italy
the rocks where the palms feel the whole world,
In Mexico a drooping mustache **"Viva"**.
Rivers dry up, love keeps quiet
and men are the harshest word
in barren squalid Anatolia.

Men are big and defeated,
an adventurous boy will heed no one
a sick man who mumbles in the splash of water
and a mad lover until daybreak
inventive, terrible and ashamed.
Useless are all the lilac trees,
men can never understand
the sadness of children born and dead,
for they die beforehand.

Because the skies grow white with blood,
there are always vanquished stars,
the diary, the sundial and the battlefield,
a face
are all that blood.

Crystal spreads its sparkle,
deathlessness, that intractable tomb,
moonlight makes the sea endure itself,
while all things pass on and go forth,
slowly gently all men die.

GÜLTEN AKIN

NOT THE FEAR OF SHIVERING

We are the tired warriors worn down by
    defeat after defeat
Too timid or ashamed to enjoy a drink
Someone gathers all the suns, keeps people
    waiting for them
It's not the fear of shivering but warming up
We are the tired warriors, so many loves
    frightened us off

They have held the mountain roads
The arrows are shot, the traps are set
Someone forgives our ugliness
In the name of friendship
We set out on flat roads again without
    arrows or rabbits
We are the daunted warriors, so many loves
    frightened us off

LAUGHING STOCK

A thousand times they made the man the
    laughing stock
They brought up fresh mirrors from below
    the ground
And held it up to the sun inside him
A thousand times they made the sun the
    laughing stock

So we could not truly gaze at the sun
Tiny and orange and pale
We knew that man to be God incalculable
Which means so chubby and stubby and pale

MOUNTAIN AIR

Someone should rip this eastern air
Off the evening and carry it to daybreak
So daylight will burst on majestic mountains
And the white dove will stretch
That's just what I said

That's just what I said this black man
Defeated and routed and weary
Should turn my steps away from the familiar street
This man to whom I say nothing more than hello
This man I detest single-track and flat
He should carry them elsewhere

I dragged my solitude like my eyes
There should be no forgetting so I did not
I a quaint sad gypsy - that serves me right -
Before the peacock's bright feathers
Aware of its ugly legs
I forcibly fixed myself and never forgot
My hands were ugly and I had no grace
It was a lie and had I believed it
I should have died eternally

That's just what I said this black man
Takes a hold of my coat in cold drinks
Takes a hold of my scarf and my boredom
He knows not my loneliness I'm not scared
He can't clutch I can't love him nor do I fear
Oh you quaint sad gypsy

A black man should take this mountain air
And carry it to majestic mountains
So day may break and the white dove grow
And a quaint sad gypsy in the waters
Should shed his defeat and decay
So daylight may burst forth

SEZAİ KARAKOÇ

FIRST

You stepped off the wrong train they flitted you
    through the city's mirror
Year in year out I watched you from the same
    window of longing
That fleeting escaping stark childish window
You used to greet graciously and matter of factly
The houses that kept getting smaller as they went
    toward the sea
You were a handful of joy in a world overflowing
    with joy

Spring knowledge sun color horse snorting and you
I am calling you come out from among the
    last virgins who are weeping
Like stone statues women come and go through
    the yellow rocks
Whichever one I look at you stir and whisper to me
    from inside
Don't stand before me move away I say it is the
    blindness of looking for the sultan
        among concubines
The blindness that lunges toward the sun and my eyes

Are you the new moon that lights up by a hand
        reaching out
Every corner of yours is embossed with drawings
        of stags
The first river that flows on deer skin
By the reaching out of a hand
I shall cry if you vanish at the entrance to the
        first street
If lilacs and scorpions turn human by looking into
        your eyes
That means Suna that you are committing the first sin
        in children's paradise
Glittering seas noiseless poems closing doors are
        carrying the meteors to you
The first arrow tested on the wrong target
Mumbles deliriously about you

KEMAL ÖZER

TO SPEAK ONE DAY

I saw the crowd, surging from the side streets,
swarmed a public square as far as the eye
        could see.
Its gaze was fastened on a single face
its ears propped to a single voice.

I saw the crowd, ready in unison
to shout a single word out of one mouth.
Poised to shoot like a tightened bow
it can barely stand in its place.

I saw the crowd, with flags in its hands
quelling its suffering and fury.
This surge of spirit does not bring together
so many arms like a fist.

I saw the crowd, unaware
of where its voice might end up.
Not for listening
but for speaking when it comes together.

ELEGY

that's a woman my mother is
a woman delayed for an overnight stay
since death revealed itself out of my
        father's hair
a woman who makes only day visits
between Scutari and Istanbul

that was my father and that was my
        father's beard
which he dipped into a lake some evening
never to pull it out again
all of his fingers whose count is forgotten
had the smell of beard

evening is a horse in all lands
a cool swarthy horse
which the children ride clinging on
        to the pillion

THE TUFT

his eyes are a sleep spread on the table
   the child scans the map
   scared on the verge of throwing up
unless he holds his mother's nearest hand

they died their lines were drawn how can he know
   they died turning a cold shoulder to death
   their lines drawn the girls and ardahan
when their eyes disappear from sleeping and weeping

is it blood which just passed it's so white
   stones and covers are all so white
is it blood which passed through the gleaming street
it's smeared all over the children's hands

every child is the clock tower of a town
   in which aerialists swing towards death
the terrible tower of the death hours
   one foot towards his mother the other
   towards death

- Ardahan: an Eastern province of Turkey

114

ALL THE KING'S MEN

you are a king how can I help recall
who could not find a place to put his hands
except the sagging shoulders of his subjects
you were the king this was certainly your right

the sea was yours the sea of plunges and hugs
when the moon stood on one side of the night
and while hairs almost reached the other hairs
yours was the night of sleeping side by side

blood is more valiant than all we have known
you reached it as if your hands had put it there
how can I help recall you were the king
your men poured out of the city's fountains

ALİ PÜSKÜLLÜOĞLU

METROPOLIS

I struggle in violent waters / most slippery of all.
Watching the big ships that sail far without me,
Abandoned, I feel foolish and ugly;
on those waters and shores where I stretch and lie
I draw things constantly.
Constantly. / Now I'm like the wild squirrels that
        take shelter
in the crevice of rocks when they know not
        where to go.

Waters flood and shroud my drawings;
but I had hoped to carry them and others into
        the future,
waters flood and shroud. / where with religious
        love my body lies,
that huge metropolis, pretty and ugly at once,
and my people with their hollow, vacuous and
        purulent eyes
waters flood and shroud / rapid and raving
waters flood and shroud and wipe out.

and again and again I keep drawing
I insist on building this metropolis.

ÖZDEMİR İNCE

IN PRAISE OF MY FATHER

I praise and exalt my father
who never left me fatherless
because he gave himself a long life.

They killed him every day
sometimes at a clerk's desk
sometimes at the grocer or the café
they killed my father every day.

My father is a set of dead fathers
getting smaller and smaller in the mirror
getting bigger and bigger in the mirror;
they claimed he trampled the sun
that he failed to see the shadow
because he said "no"
or didn't say "yes" at appropriate moments
they kept killing my father.

My father lived by dying
dying he lived long
I'm a dying son too
I praise and exalt my father.

OUR SONS

They see the backs of our sons;
we look into their eyes which are ours.

-- My son, my wounded branch!

We know our sons by the sound of their footsteps,
by their smell in the midst of countless weeds;
they smell of tobacco, fresh sweat and green grass.

-- My son, my wounded breath!

Our sons are the torrent of spring in April and May,
sometimes an eclipse, sometimes the longest day.

-- My son, my wounded waters!

The weary faces of fathers on their faces,
the sad fury of mothers on their faces;
and on their foreheads love's ineradicable seal.

-- My son, my wounded father!

Hearts cringe at dawn when the prayer call
          is chanted
the crystal mirror of inmost lives lies shattered;
the soul is in the dragon's mouth behind the
          seven hills.

-- My son, my wounded constellation!

They see the backs of our sons;
we stare into their eyes that are now a
          prison grille.

-- My son, my wounded God!

WIND, ANT, HISTORY

The wind had hanged itself on the plane tree
"Death is God's command," they said, "but why
          did he destroy himself?
he was young, brave, had a bright future,
like magic, all things good and beautiful were his."

                              It was autumn,
rain kept coming down in torrents,
an ant drenched way down to its marrows
was looking for the safety of a hole
among the fibers of the oily rope.

"Let me pass on a secret to you," said the ant
          to the rain:
"this wind didn't commit suicide, they hanged him."

HİLMİ YAVUZ

NOW FOR WHATEVER REASON

now, for whatever reason, everything
tastes like the butterfly that disintegrates

silence, as you know,
is the best-tended garden
smiles are now in exile there
pains are brothers
yet no one understands that

be it in love or in spring-deaths
all rivers give way
to engrave itself the rose
needs no apprentice or master

forgive me, children!
dip my words in the peevish salt of gray doves
then look:
has there ever been a guide worse than sorrow?

there's been none so far

but now, whatever the reason, everything
tastes like the butterfly that disintegrates

WINDY WINDOWS

windy windows! looking out of you
they were horses, there they were, plundered
                    and wrapped in
green suns of laurels they were
with deep rumps who knows from where
like a garden they appeared

windy windows! looking through you
                    and through mysteries
they were horses: wrapped in a garden
as if a light passing through the summer
                    and through deaths
like green suns they appeared

windy windows! when I look through you
green suns with deep necks, translucent,
                    shot, there
laughters with their tumultuous, untethered horses
like windy windows they appeared

windy windows! the book of a mystery
you were and sayings from summers,
                    as if,
don't ask which garden is the beginning
which horse the end? There, dead memories, carrions
they were the windy windows, I felt
and suns with green blazes on the forehead

ÜLKÜ TAMER

THE DUEL

If I am defeated, I am defeated, what does
    it matter?
Duelling you will strengthen my character.
Here I am standing in this valley up to my ankles
The flat rocks of this ground are under the soles
    of my feet,
The shrieks of the eagles traversing the sun's rails
With a grating noise blend into my forehead.
If your bullets hit my chest like the leaves of a plant
I have long forgotten about, what does it matter?

I know nothing about marksmanship, I've never used
    a revolver;
But once I face you, both dropping the cock
And failing to shoot you will harden my heart.
If I die I shall make an attractive corpse,
In a split second, hedgehogs will make their nests
    in my hair,
The snow will endeavor to shroud the rainbow
And the journalist of the dignified poverty-stricken bugs
Will take snapshots of me smiling.

HISTORY OF THE VANQUISHED

Your mouth narrates to me the history of
        the vanquished
From Bucharest and Medinah
with stories it has carried from a pillow of
        darkness.

Through your nasal passages
Roam the little leopards of the centuries
        before Christ
and of the circuses of today.

Tired soldiers stack their rifles among us,
in whispers.
On a mountain your head dips into the well
and your hair is dried in the balcony of the steppes.

Your face awaits the treaties
That will be signed overseas.

Turned toward history, your face waits and
        is awaited
by a rider wearing a shattering armor
who approaches you incessantly, inexorably,

by a rider whose shield
is going to pieces,

by that rider whose lance
is stuck in ashes

your face is expected in all the wars.

THE SPARROW

I

The world changes according to the birds' gaze

The owl that etches the mold with its sharp claws

The goldfinch that drags to its tree a fire
    its own size

The swallow whose beak forces a star to fall

The world changes according to the birds
According to the birds' gaze
And the cloud they tear up with their wings

According to the kite they marvel at
And the birdlime they covet

II

I got up from under the apricot tree at the edge
        of the courtyard
The happy child was tossing plums into the pond out
        of his window
He saw me rising toward the roof of the house
He knew my beak and feathers for sure
But he probably thought I would return

And yet I was leaving never to come back
Leaving behind the courtyard of summers,
        winters, years
The roof of insects and pips
The house of rocks
And the child's unbreakable laughter

Because the moment I'd been waiting for had arrived
The journey to the rainbow
To the point where the mountain and the
        rainbow intersect

Why I wanted this journey, I don't know
After all I don't enjoy travelling
Sleeplessness gets me down
And the tunnels in the sky scare me
But there was something in the apricot tree
        that urged me on
And when the rain stopped the rainbow dragged me
        to itself

III

The world changes according to small towns

The giant that suffers under the weight of houses
        on his back
Lets his hair grow long only in a deserted place

He extends his hand to me
Helps the birds
Offers lightness

Crossing the farm at the edge of the town
The rooster that made the hawk tired looked
        at me with love

IV

Staying in the grove is restful even for
    the sparrow

While resting in the grove the sparrow thinks of
    different things

There is no such bird as the phoenix
But sometimes that bird flies through the twilight
It is the snail of the sky
That sketches its path with gild

I thought of this while resting in the grove
As god gave voice to the phoenix
He suddenly caught sight of the nightingale
    in his palm

And then he tried black on the raven

White on the seagull

Sleep on the bat

Poetry on the pigeon

Housewife on the turtledove

Fog under the cormorant

He has tried the wet hilltops in the
    eagle's flight
And a gaze that courageously conforms
    to the beak

I thought of this while resting in the the grove
Then I came upon the answers to some of
        the questions

It is for starlings that people build the statues
(But somehow they neglect to build a
        starling statue)

To communicate with their feelings they use
        canaries

The bird they don't love without seeing is
        the vulture

V

It was late afternoon
I was supposed to reach the rainbow before sunset
The wind was waiting for me in the sky anyway
I soared
A fox stared at me in amazement
According to him I was a fox that could fly
I was a fox-sparrow according to the grove
If you ask me I was just a sparrow
It would have been wrong to loiter
Despair was beckoning me

VI

I had found the word for my journey:
Despair

VII

I saw the grief of the eagle owls and chaffinches
        and pheasants
As that day's late afternoon flapped its wings

During my flight I memorized
The lament chanted by the parrots' own tongues

Partridges and woodcocks and quails
Were weaving a white cover

I reached the rainbow at the moment
        the stars multiplied
Rolled up
Perhaps in the hollow of a tree it was waiting
        for me

The world changes according to the honor of
        the sparrows

With my beak I caught one end of the rainbow
And sprinkled some of the color fragments
        over the fields
Over meadows and roofs and chimneys
Over babies and dandelions

Then I opened it up
From one end to the other in the dark

I OFFER YOU MY THANKS

It is I who thank you, it was you who kissed me
You were the one who kissed me on my forehead
      as I slept
You made the groves nice and cool, my sparrows
      came alive;
You were a blue fox riding a blue horse,
Perhaps I had died yesterday or last week perhaps.

You were so lovely to me, so were those feet
      of yours.

METİN ALTIOK

PASSENGER

He looked every bit the traveller
Waiting
In front of the diner next to the gas station
Holding his lute and saddlebag.
The man had wafted over his shoulders at dusk
Since then his eyes reflected
The window of a bus flitting by.

SUFFERING

Suffering is the slow horse that trots back
      the distance it rode
Life's hidden and ill-omened birdlime.
It makes us taste unexpected joys
And lends color to a bird's wings.
Ripping the night open, weaving the day
It shows what simply doesn't exist as existing.

And love and happiness and others
Arrive with their feathery steps.
They don't leave their deceptive aspects to memory.
And that humane wound of ours
Blossoms forth in rose petals.
In our hearths' bleeding embroidery
It pierces the taut cloth of suffering.

ATAOL BEHRAMOĞLU

SOME DAY FOR SURE

Today first I made love, then I joined the march
I am tired, spring is here, this summer I must
        learn how to fire a gun
Books are accumulating, my hair is growing long,
        there's a tumultuous rush everywhere
I am still young, I want to see the world, kissing is
        wonderful, thinking is lovely, one day we
        shall overcome!
Some day we shall triumph for sure, I tell you,
        loan sharks of old! You geese!
        You grand vizier!
My darling is barely eighteen, we stroll on the
        boulevard, eat sandwiches and talk
        about the world
Flowers bloom all the time and wars go on, how can
        everything end with one bomb, how can those
        filthy men win
I keep thinking, I splash water on my face, I put on
        a clean shirt
One day this oppression will end, this feast for
        thieves will end
But I'm tired now, I keep smoking, I'm wearing
        a dirty raincoat
Smoke rises to the sky from the central heating
        system, there are Vietnamese books in
        my pocket
I'm thinking of my friends at the other end of
        the world, of the rivers at the other end
Quietly a girl dies there, she dies quietly
I go through the bridges, on a dark rainy day, I walk
        to the station
These houses sadden me, this ramshackle world
People and the roar of m ɔtors, the fog,
        the flowing water   ./..

What can I do... What should I do... There are dregs
        of sadness everywhere
I lean my forehead against an iron grille, those old
        days come to mind
I too was a child, naturally I was going to have
        my own loves
I think of coming back from the movies, and of my
        mother, how can everything die, how can a
        person be forgotten
Oh sky, I used to lie underneath you. Oh glittering
        fields
What can I do... What should I do... Later I read
        Descartes
My stubble gets longer, I love this girl, a short
        walk to Çankaya
Sunday, a sunny Sunday, my heart surges as I mix
        with people

A child stares out of the window, an exquisite
        child with huge dreamy eyes
Then his brother who resembles Lermontov's
        childhood photos looks out
I am writing a poem on the typewriter, I'm
        wondering about the newspapers, suddenly I hear
        the chirping of birds
I am a humble poet, my love, everything excites me
After all what is there to cry about when I catch
        sight of a common ordinary man
Looking at the man's ears, neck, eyes, eyebrows,
        and the twitches on his face
I say "The people, yes", I say "Oh child", Then I
        burst into tears
Then I put the curse on all individualistic poets and
        head for the fruit market to buy oranges
I put the curse on those effusions of words, withered
        hearts, man's salvation, etc.
I put the curse on those book worms, then I
        pardon them
I wonder how things turn out after long winter nights
All the things told in tales after those long
        winter nights   ./..

From time to time I pause to think about these,
        a sadness comes in the wake of a joy
My heart is a spring sky with all its fiddle faddle.
        In short a heart in the Turkish language
Waiting is so wearying, here and there I talk about
        a lot of things in a mad rush
I take a bus, I scrutinize an insect holding it
        by its wings
In the past I used to walk in springtime to regions
        where there were ruins and meadows
Reminded of that old American's poem, that poem
        about autumn
There were meadows in the poem, reminiscent of
        spring to be sure
This way I get ready for a new passion, for dashing
        out into the streets again
To throw myself headlong off a precipice
The image of something big and blue lingers in my
        mind, it's probably from a film I had seen
A hat, a sky in a flurry, a warm spurious world
I keep talking and telling stories, but there is no end
        to my homesickness
I can squander all my loves in a split second, I am
        reminded of those rain-drenched roads
Smell of gasoline, damp poles, my father's fat and
        warm like a loaf of bread
I used to sleep. Suddenly you notice there's a new
        feature film at the movie theater, a new girl
        in town, a new waiter at the café
He stood on the balcony sad, dressed in his robe...
Now why should this sadden me, why is this
        heart-rending, why all this dithering
As if I am going to die tomorrow or the police
        will storm in soon
To impound my books, my typewriter, this poem,
        my darling's photo hanging on the wall

To ask what's your father's name, where you
        were born, would you kindly come
        to the precinct
I'm thinking of my friends at the other end of
        the world, of the rivers at the other end   ./..

134

Quietly a girl dies there, she is dying quietly
     in Vietnam
Weeping I draw the picture of a heart in the air
I wake crying, one day we shall defeat them
     for sure!
Some day we shall triumph, I tell you, importers,
     exporters, I tell you, Islam's Chief Dignitary!
We shall overcome for sure! One day we shall
     emerge victorious! We are going to repeat this
     a thousand times!
Then we shall multiply it a thousand times and
     then a thousand times again with anthems
I and my darling and my friend shall march
     in the boulevards
We shall march with the gushing joy of being
     created anew
We shall march, increasing and multiplying
     as we go...

IF I DIE, I'LL DIE IN EARLY EVENING

If I die, I'll die in early evening
Pitchblack snow will fall on the city
My heart will blanket the roads
Through my fingers
I shall see the night descending

If I die, I'll die in early evening
Children will go to the movies
Burying my face in a flower
I want to cry and all that
Deep down a train passes

If I die, I'll die in early evening
Taken over by the urge to walk away from it all
I will enter a city one evening
Through the apricot trees
I shall go and gaze at the sea
And watch a theatrical show

If I die, I'll die in early evening
A cloud will flit in the distance
The cloud of a murky childhood
A surrealist painter
Will begin to transform the world
Bird songs and screams
The colors of the sea and of meadows
Will intermingle

I'll bring you a poem
Whose words gush out of my dreams
The world will split into my parts
A Sunday morning in one of them
A sky in another
Yellow leaves in one
A man in another
Will start everything all over again

SENNUR SEZER

AILING

I

Loving hard is easy. To stand on the gallows and
to swear.

Suffering grows, doesn't get less! Women always keep
after their children barefooted. Women at
windows. To write all the cheap complaints.
But the way out...

Night grows in the palms of beggars. Sweaty palms of
youths with fresh mustaches. Their blushing
bashful age gets old with a smile.
Smiles never age.

And it's as if someone gets born somewhere
in the night!

II

A human first loves himself. Sketches his hands and
eyes on a rock. To write of his love he places
three branches and gets stoned.

What we craft is a great song. Each melody has lasted
a hundred years. Its end is a tale. What we
craft is a great song if only it could last
long after us...

It was I who first put the three branches into the void.

İSMET ÖZEL

A SHROUD FOR MY DARLING

The shrine of a woman whose hair blazes in henna
soars overhead in an undertone
these violet autumn days inflict their madness
driving you out of your senses and books
tumors, dead ants
chills and shivers cover me
curiosity
is the genesis of a revolutionary
and above me in an undertone fly
cancer, begonia, death.

White gauze behind the windowpane
and eyes plucked out
real human eyes heavy like rocks
a mother endures all the agony
and the dust stirred up by her corpse,
you warden of anguish, you autumn days.

Under the rain of the rebel leader
I clobber my own scorched and paltry beauty
Saturday afternoons pierce like a cramp
my hope
is a ferocious animal
which keeps toppling the banknotes and mass meetings
and chokes the houses we live in
with the aroma of cinnamon and with weariness,
curiosity
is the genesis of a revolutionary
in the bazaars some coppersmiths wash
and women who knead dough are dragged with clangs
in their mortars they pound their stubborn streak
and their vile hopes too.

I cannot love a girl secretly
a thousand curiosities prick me all over
those gloomy smells of incense our mothers
craving food in pregnancy must eat dirt
unite the ropes of my heart against the moon
my heavenly pain throbs in my wrists
sawdust convulsing sawdust
sawdust of the sledge that beats on my temples.

REFİK DURBAŞ

ITS GRIEF

with this furious face in the old days
I used to transport wooden birds
to my mouth's country which grew feathers
each night the dead with the dead
I carried this diminishing face of mine

those birds used to be my knife
because I went hunting with them
if I had to water my dead ones with blood
if dust whirled around my neck
I swear to god that's how I hunted

in truth it is the way a wooden bird
takes wing on our forehead
before death lays siege with knives
on our grief-stricken sky
death is the way love takes wing

SPARROWS

Dashed out into the street. Morning
roamed the city from one end to the other
Broke all the windowpanes
shifted the streets around
the place of sadness in the heart
the address of solitude

Sparrows fluttered in your hair
spared only those sparrows

ELEGY

Ox carts glided through the mountains
At night. Time suckled by the wind
rifle and faith, hope and bullet shells
and the bright hearts of the rebel bands
To make rain on the dawn of independence
You snatched victory from the flying birds.
And now from those days of light,
they have plundered young deaths
and with ox carts through the mountains
still flows the poetry
of love, sweat of the brow, and suffering.

BIOGRAPHICAL NOTES
(In Alphabetical Order)

GÜLTEN AKIN (b. 1933) is Turkey's leading woman poet. After receiving her law degree from the University of Ankara, she worked as a teacher and practiced law in several Anatolian towns where her husband served as a provincial administrator. Later she joined the staff of the Turkish Language Society in Ankara. In addition to eight collections of poems, she has published several short plays. In 1965 one of her poetry books won the coveted prize of the Turkish Language Society.

SABAHATTİN KUDRET AKSAL (b. 1920) is a versatile writer who has received major awards for his poetry, plays, and short stories. He holds a degree in philosophy from the University of Istanbul. In the 1940s he taught philosophy in some private schools. Later he worked as a Ministry of Labor inspector and held several top posts with the Municipality of Istanbul, including Director of the City Conservatory and the Municipal Theaters. He is now retired. Many of his plays have been published and produced.

METİN ALTIOK (b. 1941) worked as a journalist and editor after studying philosophy at the University of Ankara. He has published three books of poetry.

MELİH CEVDET ANDAY (b. 1915) is one of Turkey's prominent literary figures. He enjoys fame as a poet, playwright, novelist, essayist, and translator. From 1936 to 1938 he studied sociology in Brussels. Later he worked as a consultant for the Publications Division of the Ministry of Public Education and as a librarian at the Ankara Library. Since the 1970s he has been writing a weekly column for the Istanbul daily **Cumhuriyet.** From 1954 until the late 1970s he taught diction and dramatic literature at the City Conservatory of Istanbul. His work has been translated into many languages. In 1971 UNESCO honored him as one of the world's major literary figures. Anday has won many of Turkey's top awards.

AHMET ARİF (b. 1925) is a best-selling poet who makes his living as a journalist. Ahmet Arif has published only one book of poems: It has gone through many printings and has sold an estimated thirty-thousand copies.

ECE AYHAN (b. 1931), a graduate of the Faculty of Political Science (Ankara), worked as a provincial administrator before becoming an editor. One of Turkey's most innovative and controversial poets, he has published seven collections and a diary.

ATAOL BEHRAMOĞLU (b. 1942) holds a degree in Russian language and literature from the University of Ankara. He made his living as a translator and editor. Later he worked for the City Theaters of Istanbul and as an editor of the leftist magazine **Militan.** In the 1980s he was forced to live outside of Turkey. In 1982 he won the International Prize of the **Lotus** magazine. He has published many collections of his poems and translations.

İLHAN BERK (b. 1916) has been a vital force in the modernization of Turkish poetry since the 1940s. He has published about twenty volumes of poetry and has compiled several major anthologies. He has also published some major essays which have stirred extensive debate.

SALAH BİRSEL (b. 1919) is a versatile writer who has published poetry, essays, translations, a novel, and treatises on poetry and painting. A graduate of the Department of Philosophy at the University of Istanbul, he has been a teacher of French, a labor inspector, and editor-in-chief of the publications division of the Turkish Language Society. He is one of Turkey's most successful essayists.

NECATİ CUMALI (b. 1921) is a prolific writer of novels, short stories, essays and plays as well as a prominent poet. After graduating from the Faculty of Law at the University of Ankara he practised law for some years. Since the late 1950s he has been an independent writer, and has lived in Paris, Israel, and Istanbul. He is the recipient of Turkey's most prestigious literary awards.

CEVAT ÇAPAN (b. 1933) is a Professor of English Literature and drama at Mimar Sinan University in Istanbul. He is a celebrated translator of poetry. His own poems have been collected in one volume.

FAZIL HÜSNÜ DAĞLARCA (b. 1914) was honored by a panel of Turkish men of letters as "Turkey's leading living poet" in 1967, and received the award of the International Poetry Forum (Pittsburgh, Pa.) He has published about seventy books of poetry. Dağlarca's books have also been published in French, Macedonian, Estonian, German, and English. In 1974 he received Yugoslavia's Golden Wreath Award and in 1977 he was named poet of the year at Rotterdam Poetry International.

ARİF DAMAR (b. 1925) has published eight collections of poems, one of which won the prestigious Yeditepe Award. For some years he owned and operated a bookstore.

REFİK DURBAŞ (b. 1944) has been on the staff of several newspapers, and currently works for **Cumhuriyet.** He has published seven books of poetry, one of which won the Yeditepe Award.

ATTİLA İLHAN (b. 1925), a major figure of Turkish literature, has achieved impressive success in many genres - poetry, fiction, essays, travel writing, film scripts, etc. He has also been a columnist and editor of books and literary journals. He has won many top awards.

ÖZDEMİR İNCE (b. 1936) studied French literature and worked some years as a teacher of French. Later he served as program director at the Turkish Radio and TV Administration. He has published many volumes of his own poems, critical writing, and translations. Three books of his selected poems have been published in Greek, French and Bulgarian. He has been elected to membership in the Académie Mallarmé (Paris).

SEZAİ KARAKOÇ (b. 1933) is a graduate of the Faculty of Political Science (Ankara). After serving as an official of the Ministry of Finance, he became a columnist in Istanbul and has been the editor of several periodicals. In addition to many books of poems, he has written various monographs on literature and culture.

CAHİT KÜLEBİ (b. 1917) taught literature, served as Turkey's educational attaché in Switzerland, and was a deputy under-secretary for cultural affairs. He ranks as one of his country's leading poets. For many years, he was editor-in-chief and secretary general of the Turkish Language Society.

AHMET OKTAY (b. 1933) is an award-winning poet who has published many books of poetry, literary essays, and cultural treatises. A play he wrote was produced in 1974. He is currently one of the top editors of the Istanbul daily **Milliyet** and has served as the host of a "books programme" on Turkish Television.

İSMET ÖZEL (b. 1944) holds a degree in French Language and Literature from the University of Ankara and works as a teacher of French at the State Conservatory in Istanbul. He has published many collections of poems as well as critical studies of poetry.

KEMAL ÖZER (b. 1935) has been the editor of several literary journals and once operated a bookshop in Istanbul. In addition to many volumes of his own poetry, he has translated Hungarian and Bulgarian poetry into Turkish. He is currently editor-in-chief of **Varlık**, Turkey's oldest literary magazine (since 1933). In 1976 he won the Poetry Award of the Turkish Language Society.

ALİ PÜSKÜLLÜOĞLU (b. 1935) is an award-winning writer of children's literature and an indefatigable compiler of anthologies and dictionaries. He has published five books of poetry and served as editor of literary magazines. For many years he was on the staff of the Turkish Language Society.

SENNUR SEZER (b. 1943), after working as a bookkeeper and editorial assistant for **Varlık**, became a writer for the daily **Cumhuriyet**. She has published six poetry books and a children's book.

CEMAL SÜREYA (b. 1931) held various positions in the Turkish Ministry of Finance (including Director of the Istanbul Mint) after graduation from the Faculty of Political Science (Ankara). He has received two major awards for his poetry. Between 1960 and 1970 he served twice as editor-in-chief of the influential journal **Papirüs.** He enjoys fame as an essayist, critic, anthologist, and translator as well.

ÜLKÜ TAMER (b. 1937) was educated at Robert College (Istanbul) and the Journalism Institute at the University of Istanbul. He has won awards for his poetry and for his translation of Edith Hamilton's **Mythology.** In addition to numerous collections of his own poems, he has published more than a hundred books in translation. He is currently a consultant for the cultural programmes of the Turkish Radio and Television Administration.

HİLMİ YAVUZ (b. 1936) worked for some years as a journalist and editor. Later he served on the staff of the Turkish Desk at BBC. He holds an advanced degree in philosophy from the University of London and has been on the faculty of two universities in Istanbul. In addition to several collections of poems, he has published numerous volumes of criticism. He is currently Chief Cultural Advisor to the Major of Istanbul.

CAN YÜCEL (b. 1926) studied Greek and Latin at the University of Ankara and pursued further studies at Cambridge University. He later worked for the Turkish Desk at BBC. Some of his poems, particularly his short satires, have been widely popular. Because of his strongly critical poems he has been imprisoned several times. Yücel is also one of Turkey's most prominent translators.

EDITOR

TALAT S. HALMAN, the editor and translator of **Living Poets of Turkey,** is one of the leading translators of Turkish literature into English. His work has been extensively published in the English-speaking world. In 1986, the Translation Center of Columbia University awarded him the "Thornton Wilder Prize". His books in English include **Contemporary Turkish Literature,** two volumes on the poetry of 13th Century mystic Yunus Emre, **Modern Turkish Drama,** a collection of his original poems entitled **Shadows of Love / Les ombres de l'amour** (with French translations by Louise Gareau-Des Bois), **Süleyman the Magnificent - Poet, Mevlana Celaleddin Rumi and the Whirling Dervishes** (with Metin And), **Rain One Step Away: Selected Poems of Melih Cevdet Anday** (with Brian Swann), **Selected Poems of Fazıl Hüsnü Dağlarca, I am Listening to Istanbul: Selected Poems of Orhan Veli Kanık, A Dot on the Map: Selected Stories and Poems by Sait Faik,** and many other books.

He is a poet who has published four collections in Turkish. His translations into Turkish include the complete sonnets of Shakespeare, selected poetry of Wallace Stevens and Langston Hughes, the fiction of William Faulkner and Mark Twain, Eugene O'Neill's "The Iceman Cometh" and Robinson Jeffers' adaptation of Euripides' "Medea", a book of Eskimo poetry, a volume of ancient Egyptian poetry, and a massive anthology of the poetry of ancient civilizations.

His articles on Turkish culture and literature have been published in scores of encyclopedias, anthologies, journals, etc. in the English-speaking world.

Currently he is a professor of Turkish language and literature at New York University. Previously he served on the faculties of Columbia University, the University of Pennsylvania, and Princeton University for many years.

In 1988 Bosphorus University awarded him an honorary doctorate for his contributions to Turkish culture and literature. He received the Rockefeller Fellowship in the Humanities in 1989.

In 1971 he became Turkey's Minister of Culture (the first person ever to hold this cabinet post) and created the Ministry. From 1980 to 1982 he served as Turkey's Ambassador for Cultural Affairs, the first and still the only person to have held this post. He was also Turkey's Deputy Permanent Representative at the United Nations.

Some of his books have been translated into Persian, French, Hindi, Hebrew, and Urdu.

His translation of Güngör Dilmen's one-woman play "I, Anatolia" was performed by the prominent actress Yıldız Kenter in London's Royal Festival Hall, New York's Lincoln Center, Moscow, Istanbul and Ankara. His one-man Shakespeare program entitled "Heroes and Clowns" enjoyed success in Istanbul and Ankara where it was presented by the leading actor Müşfik Kenter.

He is a member of the Poetry Society of America, The Academy of American Poets, The American Center of P.E.N. (where he was on the Executive Board from 1974 to 1981 and now serves on the Translation Committee), The American Literary Translators Association, The International Committee for Poetry, and other literary and academic societies.

In 1971 Queen Elizabeth conferred upon him the title of "Knight Grand Cross, G.B.E., The Most Excellent Order of the British Empire."

FURTHER READING

The poetry of the Turkish Republic has had little recognition in the English-speaking world. Until the late 1950s fewer than 200 modern Turkish poems had been published in English translation. Since then, however, translation activity, although hardly brisk, has gained momentum. There are now some general anthologies and many books featuring the selected poems of individual poets.

For readers interested in acquiring a well-balanced understanding of Turkish poetry from the late 13th Century to the present day, there is an excellent anthology: Nermin Menemencioğlu (in collaboration with Fahir İz): **The Penguin Book of Turkish Verse,** 1978.

Another useful collection comprises short stories and poetry: Talat Sait Halman: **Contemporary Turkish Literature,** Associated University Presses, 1982.

There are numerous volumes featuring the work of Nazım Hikmet (1902-1963), the most influential Turkish modernist. The first collection simply entitled **Poems** was published by Masses and Mainstream, New York, in 1954. The translator's name Ali Yunus is a pseudonym for two women, Nilüfer Mizanoğlu Reddy and Rosette Avigdor Coryell.

The Cypriot-Turkish-British poet Taner Baybars published three volumes of Nazım Hikmet's selected poems in his versions: **Selected Poems,** 1967; **The Moscow Symphony,** 1970; **The Day Before Tomorrow,** 1972, all three published in England.

From the late 1970s to the late 1980s, Randy Blasing and Mutlu Konuk produced many volumes devoted to the work of Nazım Hikmet, mostly published by Persea Books of New York. These include **Things I Didn't Know I Loved, The Epic of Sheik Bedreddin, Human Landscapes, Rubaiyat,** and **Selected Poems.**

The first and still only bi-lingual book of Turkish poetry came out in 1969 - **Fazıl Hüsnü Dağlarca: Selected Poems,** translated by Talat Sait Halman, Pittsburgh University Press.

Cross-Cultural Communications (Merrick, New York) is planning to publish ten bi-lingual books, each featuring the work of an individual modern Turkish poet. The first group of four will be devoted to the work of İlhan Berk, Fazıl Hüsnü Dağlarca, Talat Sait Halman, and Kemal Özer, all translated by Halman. In 1980, the same publisher produced a chapbook entitled **The Bird and I,** (selected poems of Fazıl Hüsnü Dağlarca), and in 1988 released an audio-cassette, recorded by Halman, with all of the poems in the chapbook and many other poems.

Orhan Veli Kanık (1914-1950) has generated some interest in the United States. 1971 saw the publication of **I am Listening to Istanbul: Selected Poems of Orhan Veli Kanık,** Corinth Books, New York, translated by Talat Sait Halman. In 1988 Erje Ayden published a chapbook of his translations of 17 poems by Kanık, Geronimo Books, New York. The chapbook is entitled "The Covered Bazaar". 1989 saw the publication of **I, Orhan Veli,** Hanging Loose Press, translated by Murat Nemet-Nejat.

The selected poems of Melih Cevdet Anday are available in **On the Nomad Sea,** a chapbook, translations by Nermin Menemencioğlu and Talat Sait Halman, and a book entitled **Rain One Step Away,** The Charioteer Press, Washington DC, 1980, translated by Talat Sait Halman and Brian Swann.

A fairly large group of poems, mainly from the modern period, are featured in Derek Patmore's **The Star and the Crescent: An Anthology of Modern Turkish Poetry,** Constable and Co., London, 1945.

A very interesting critical essay is "Modern Turkish Poetry" (by Prof. Orhan Burian), published (anonymously) in pamphlet form by the Turkish Information Office, New York, 1950.

Several journals have devoted special sections to or produced special issues of Turkish literature (some exclusively poetry):

Western Review, edited by Nermin Menemencioğlu. **Core,** edited by Feyyaz Kayacan and Mevlüt Ceylan. **Frank International,** edited by Edouard Roditi. **Zenos,** edited by Feyyaz Kayacan.

The Literary Review, edited by Clarence R. Decker.

Modern Poetry in Translation, edited by Osman Türkay and Taner Baybars.

The Literary Review, Review of National Literatures, Mundus Artium, Contemporary Literature in Translation, The Greenfield Review, Literature East and West, the new renaissance, The Bulletin of the Poetry Society of America, and **Translation: The Journal of Literary Translation,** all edited by Talat Sait Halman. Also "Greek and Turkish Poets of Today", special issue of **The Pacific Quarterly,** edited by Yannis Goumas and T. S. Halman.

Useful survey articles may be found in **The Encyclopedia of Poetry and Poetics, Encyclopedia Britannica, The Encyclopedia of Islam, The Encyclopedia of World Literature in the Twentieth Century,** and the **Columbia Dictionary of Modern European Literature.**

New Writing from the Middle East, ed. Leo Hamalian and John D. Yohannan, New York, New American Library, 1978, has a very good section on Turkish literature with selections from the work of many prominent poets.

Some interesting versions of mid-century poems may be found in Lawrence E. Patterson: "Contemporary Turkish Poetry", **The Poetry Book Magazine,** Vo. V, No. 3, 1953.

BOOKS EDITED BY DOST PUBLICATIONS

TURKISH MINIATURE PAINTING by Metin And
The Ottoman Period. 68 miniatures in full color and 107 black and white illustrations, 17x23.5, 142 pages, English............................. $ 10.-

KARAGÖZ - Turkish Shadow Theatre by Metin And
98 full color and 160 black and white illustrations, 17x23.5, hard cover, 118 pages, English. .... $ 12.-

TURKISH DANCING by Metin And
A Pictorial History of Turkish Dancing. From folk dancing to whirling dervishes, belly dancing to ballet. With 194 illustrations, 101 in color, 19.5x26.5, 182 pages, English.. $ 10.-

MEVLANA CELALEDDİN RUMİ AND THE WHIRLING DERVISHES by Talat S. Halman & Metin And
Sufi philosophy, whirling rituals, poems of ecstasy, miniature paintings. 33 full color and 30 black and white illustrations, 20x27.5, hard cover, 112 pages, English.. $ 12.-

SÜLEYMAN THE MAGNIFICENT, POET
30 poems by Süleyman the Magnificent, translated into English by Talat S. Halman with an introduction by Esin Atıl. 11 miniatures and paintings in color, 17x23.5, hard cover, 88 pages......................... $ 15.-

NASREDDİN HOCA Told by Aziz Nesin
Retold in English by Talat S. Halman, illustrations by Zeki Fındıkoğlu. 40 illustrations in full color, 17x23.5, 120 pages......................... $ 10.-

THE BLUE PARADISE OF LYCIA by Temuçin Aygen
With color photographs and maps of ancient cities, 17x23.5, 120 pages, English... $ 10.-

SELECTION OF 33 TURKISH MINIATURES by Metin And
The Ottoman Period. 33 color plates, 33x47, hard cover, 72 pages, English, German... $ 40.-

TURKISH MINIATURES ALBUM (I, II, III)
6 posters in full color, 35x50. Each .... $ 10.-

TURKISH CALLIGRAPHY ALBUM (V)
6 posters in full color, 35x50. .... $ 10.-

ALBUM C-1, 2, 3, 4 (Istanbul Engravings 1840, Turkish Miniatures, Turkish Calligraphy, Mevlana Celaleddin Rumi)
6 posters in color, 25x35. Each .... $ 7.-